"I didn't realize that talking about food and cooking could make me laugh and cry at the same time until I read *Embrace Your Southern, Sugar!* Julia's thoughts on Southern culture brought on a fit of laughter and nostalgia. Most of all, Julia reaffirms our Southern pride."

♥ *Gerald McRaney*

EMMY AWARD–WINNING ACTOR AND
MISSISSIPPI NATIVE

"Julia hit the nail on the head with her latest knee slappin', laugh-out-loud, charming book. Being from Atlanta, Georgia, I can't disagree: our good-byes take longer than a Sunday church sermon and turning down seconds to any home-cooked meal is disrespectful. I absolutely love that Julia shared her favorite Southern recipes because I now reside in Los Angeles and 'when I can't get back home, I [also] eat home.' This book certainly delivers."

♥ *Finesse Mitchell*

ACTOR, AUTHOR, *SATURDAY NIGHT LIVE* ALUM, AND STAND-UP COMEDIAN

Embrace Your Southern, Sugar!

Embrace Your Southern, Sugar!

JULIA FOWLER

GIBBS SMITH
TO ENRICH AND INSPIRE HUMANKIND

❤ *This book is dedicated to Granny Winnie,*
Papa Cooter, Granny Fowler,
and Papa Fowler. Your love, humor, and
Southernness are forever monogrammed on
my heart. I miss y'all every dadgum day.

First Edition

24 23 22 21 20   5 4 3 2 1

Published by
Gibbs Smith
P.O. Box 667
Layton, Utah 84041

1.800.835.4993 orders
www.gibbs-smith.com

Designed by Katie Jennings

Printed and bound in China

Gibbs Smith books are printed on either recycled, 100% post-consumer waste,
FSC-certified papers or on paper produced from sustainable PEFC-certified forest/
controlled wood source. Learn more at www.pefc.org.

Library of Congress Cataloging-in-Publication Data
Names: Fowler, Julia, 1971- author.
Title: Embrace your Southern, Sugar! / Julia Fowler.
Description: First edition. | Layton, Utah : Gibbs Smith, [2020] | Summary:
  "Ms. Julia Fowler is back, and this time she's goin' to talk her lipstick off about even
  more all-things-Southern"-- Provided by publisher.
Identifiers: LCCN 2019054601 | ISBN 9781423653998 (hardcover) | ISBN
  9781423654001 (epub)
Subjects: LCSH: American wit and humor--Southern States. | Southern
  States--Humor. | Southern States--Social life and customs--Humor. |
  Southern States--Quotations, maxims, etc. | LCGFT: Humor. | Quotations.
Classification: LCC PN6231.S64 F69 2020 | DDC 818/.602--dc23
LC record available at https://lccn.loc.gov/2019054601

CONTENTS

Introduction 7

Embrace Comin' and Goin' 11

Embrace the Dadblame Weather 37

Embrace Your Obsession with Football 61

Embrace Your Southern Fried Palate 85

Embrace Your Health 115

Embrace Bein' Country 141

Acknowledgments 166

Introduction

WELL, BLESS Y'ALL'S HEARTS! It seems my first book, *Talk Southern to Me*, made y'all grin like a rooster in a hen house, so the good folks over at Gibbs Smith Publisher asked if I wanted to write a sequel. Is a ten-pound robin fat? Does Martha White make a mean biscuit? Is a frog's butt watertight? Sho'nuff! I'm plumb tickled to death to keep talkin' Southern to y'all, and if that's not a fact, then God's a possum.

Birthing my first book was a fascinating journey—kinda like birthing a baby, I reckon. I once heard comedian Carol Burnett say, "Giving birth is like taking your bottom lip and forcing it over your entire head." Perhaps this is why I never had youngins. In any case, while birthing *Talk Southern to Me* was a challenge, I found it significantly less painful than Carol Burnett's description of childbirth. So I licked the calf again—even though climbing a mountain of blank pages is more terrifying than strolling into church late on Easter Sunday.

Now for youins who missed my first book or have never seen the videos on my YouTube Southern Women Channel—let me get y'all up to speed. I was born and raised in Gaffney, South Carolina, and graduated from the University of South Carolina. The truth is, I always took my Southernness for granted. I never really thought about it much. It wasn't until I began pursuing a career in show business, and found myself living outside of the South in both New York City and Los Angeles, that I realized just how Southern I am. And just how many hearts needed blessing. Many highfalutin showbiz folks warned that my Southernness would be an obstacle to success. Bless 'em. I've found the opposite to be true. I've found that being Southern is not only a privilege, it's my greatest asset. I proudly embrace my Southern.

Despite umpteen gajillion voice and diction classes, I still *choose* to speak in my native Southern accent. Yes, I can lose it in a second. But why would I? I enjoy confusing non-Southerners by speaking Southernese like, "Shootfire, come Friday week I'm gonna give that idjut a whatfor and down the road." Which means next Friday I'm gonna have a come-to-Jesus meetin' with an idiot. Still confused? It means we're gonna have a heated conversation.

The thing is, not only do I talk Southern, I also write Southern. Which can be a hitch in your giddy up when trying to peddle projects in Hollywood, 'cause most of the bigwigs in La La Land don't speak Southernese. So, I decided to make a video for YouTube. I gathered some of my talented Southern girlfriends and made a video called *Sh%t Southern Women Say*. Our first video went viral in twenty-four hours, and that's how the Southern Women Channel was born. Years later, it's a hobby gone wild. Even though we're all busy with our separate careers, we still get a hoot and holler outta making YouTube videos, and the channel now has more than twenty-three million views.

I'm forever grateful to the devoted fans of Southern Women Channel and for all the love my first book received. I get such a kick out of celebrating Southern language and culture. We Southerners are a particular bunch who have our own sense of style, prescribe to our own code of etiquette, and can craft an insult dripping in so much honey you'd think we're giving you a compliment. *Well, sweetie pie, I couldn't pull that off, but look at you!*

This book is another love letter to the South. It explores eccentric Southern traits not covered in my previous book. As you read, I hope you conjure joyful memories of all the Southerners who have graced your life. If you're not from the South, I hope to learn ya a thing or two that you can tote back into your own culture. If you are from the South, then you better go call your Mama and 'nem and thank 'em for your Southern raising. Thank them for teaching you the art of Southern charm and to speak the Southern tongue. Thank them for guiding your life with homespun Southern philosophies like, "An ounce of pretension is worth a pound of manure." There's nothing purdier in this world than authenticity.

Embrace Your Southern, Sugar!

Embrace
Comin’ and Goin’

Comin' and Goin'

"Hey Sugarbritches!"

SOUTHERNERS ARE NOT STEALTHY CREATURES. You can hear us coming from a mile away.

"Well, fry my feet and call 'em drumsticks! Lookahere what the cat drug in! Mercy days, I haven't seen you since you were knee high to a grasshopper! Let me hug your neck, darlin'. [Insert neck hug.] Lord, look at you all grown up and prettier than a pie supper. How's your Mama and 'nem?" This is a standard Southern greeting. This is part of Southern hospitality. No matter where you go in the South, you'll find that we Southerners take our time. We take our time with meals, on Sunday afternoon drives, and especially in conversation. You could paint an entire house in the amount of time it takes a Southerner to say, "Hello."

But a proper Southerner would never just say, "Hello." How tacky. And as I explained in my previous book, there's nothing tackier than being tacky. You will never catch a Southerner saying, "Hi, how are you guys?" Or "Hello, you all." No. No. No. "Hey, y'all!" is the customary way to greet a group of folks in the South. And when greeting an individual, you can bet your Granny's china we're gonna lavish you with a honeysuckled term of endearment like, "Hey, sweet pea!" "Hey honey pie!" or "Hey, sugar!" Southerners spit more sugar out of their mouths than a Dixie Crystals sugar shaker.

After drizzling you with a honeyed "Heeeeey," a Southerner then feels compelled to qualify their enthusiasm and surprise at bumping into you with phrases like, "Well, cut off my legs and call me shorty! Running into you makes me happier than a pup with two tails. How are yewwwww?" Then, of course, a full-fledged chewing-the-fat session follows, which can take forevah and evah. Growing up, I had to take a sleeping bag with me in case my Mama ran into somebody she knew at the grocery store. If they gave an Olympic gold medal for talking, Mama would be on a box of Wheaties. But she can't help it. Her Mama, my Granny Winnie, could also talk the ears off a hobby horse. She had a vivacious personality and always made a big show out of greeting folks. Like most Southerners, Granny Winnie never met a stranger.

I was raised by these Southern women, so I also spew saccharine salutations and have long-winded conversations with people I run into. And I've been trained like a dog to speak to people I don't know because Mama insists "it's the polite thing to do." But this sort of wild and crazy behavior will elicit some serious sideways glances outside of the South. When you flash a toothy smile to a stranger in New York City and say, "Hey, how are yewwww?" it confuses them and makes them suspicious. They tend to clutch their purse or slink away assuming you are coo-coo-ca-choo. So, this became my favorite game when I lived in NYC. I would trudge through the crowded city streets and attempt to get the miserable, black-clad, rushed souls to smile and return my enthusiastic greetings. I considered it a victory both for myself and Southern culture if I could score even one toothless grin.

After moving to Los Angeles, I learned that people on the West Coast don't really take time to properly greet each other either. In general,

In the South, we kill 'em with kindness.

the LA philosophy is, "If you can't help my career then I don't have time to chitchat." But this does not deter my Southern spirit. I still smile and greet people with gusto. I force folks to linger in conversation far longer than they would prefer 'cause I can't do one ding-dong thing to make them famous. I whip out "darlin'," "hun," and "sugar" more often than Cali gals whip out "like." My Southern accent and grammar choices often get mocked in LA But *like* at least I don't *like* say *like* every other word. And at least I introduce myself with a firm handshake and my full name. Southerners are taught from a young age that introducing yourself with a firm handshake and your full name is not only proper etiquette, it also radiates confidence. This is how it's done, huns. A limp handshake is guaran-dang-teed to make a terrible first impression, and dishrag handshakes are one of California's natural resources. Bless their hearts.

Speaking of heart blessing, which is an art form I schooled y'all on in *Talk Southern to Me*, don't ever assume that just because a Southerner takes the time to greet you that they actually like you. In the South, we kill 'em with kindness. The classic Southern

I despise you greeting is, "Heeeeey, nice to see you." Short. Simple. Not too sweet. As a teenager, it would infuriate me when Mama would make me speak to someone I didn't like or who I knew didn't like me. But as an adult, I embrace this useful Southern skill. It forces me to act like a lady when I would rather jack jaws. Charm disarms an enemy. In addition, never assume a Southerner remembers you when they greet you. I have exchanged excited hugs and had a twenty-minute conversation with a lady, then, after she walked away, wondered, "Who in the Sam Bell Hill was that?" It never occurred to me to admit to her that I didn't remember her. That would have been rude. So, the mystery continues.

COMIN' INTO THIS WORLD

Perhaps the reason Southerners greet folks in such an over-the-top fashion is because we come into this world in a showy fashion. First, there's the public pregnancy announcement. In the age of social media, this has become even more competitive, with creative professional photo shoots and some downright bizarre sonogram reveals. I'm surprised Facebook hasn't created new community standards concerning Southern sonograms. And expecting Southern mamas spend countless hours agonizing over nursery decor as if it's scientifically proven an infant is certain to die a violent crib death unless they are sleeping on monogrammed statement sheets, under a hand-painted mural that perfectly ties together the nursery's celestial, nautical, animal, princess, or race-car theme.

Then come the extravagant baby showers, which require theme colors, fancy invitations, decorative diaper cake centerpieces, homemade edible cake, finger sandwiches, deviled eggs, punch, and enough butter mints to feed the state of Texas. It's a good thing butter mints don't induce labor, or else there would be hordes of Southern mamas suddenly droppin' babies in church basements and country clubs, clad in stylish lace maternity dresses accessorized to a T. Southern women dress up to go to the post office, so of course we get gussied up to celebrate a new Southerner coming into this world. I once showed up to a baby shower in NYC dressed in the Southern shower uniform: sundress, heels, pearls, and bright lipstick. Everyone else was wearing jeans and ChapStick. The menu consisted of bagels, salad, and more salad. And many guests did not stay to watch the mother open her gifts. Blasphemy! I "ooohhhed" and "ahhhhhed" over onesies and burp cloths and gave plenty of "Isn't that precious," only to get my feelings hurt when my gift, a monogrammed baby blanket, did not receive a grandiose reaction. I considered calling Child Protective Services, as I felt compelled to safeguard this unborn child from a mama who did not appreciate an embroidered monogram.

Then there is the birth itself. Even if a Southern mama spends forty-eight hours in grueling labor, she's still likely to put her face on and get her hair fixed before posing for that iconic hospital bed "Mama and fresh-out-of-the-oven baby" picture. Move over Kate Middleton and Meghan Markle . . . nobody presents post-childbirth better than a Southern woman. Oh, and you better believe that both baby and mama must have stylish "coming home from the hospital" outfits just in case the fashion police are staked out in the hospital parking lot.

And finally, the formal baby announcement itself can rival a wedding invitation in its elegance, because announcing a Southern baby's name is a big fat deal. We don't come into this world with ordinary names. The South is filled with unique names, such as Aberdean,

Cleavon, Verdi, and Dynell. We also don't spell names in ordinary ways. Katelin might be spelled Caitlin. Or Kaytlynn. Or Caytlin. And we also have a tendency to use surnames, such as Finley, Marshall, Campbell, or Bellamy as first names.

Oftentimes, one name is not enough. Why settle on one when you can show double love with names like Betty Merle, Mary Lane, or John David? And we love to incorporate family names. My Louisiana pal Delaine was named after her mama whose first name is also guess what—Delaine. My Mississippi friend Katherine's middle name is "Dement"—her grandmother's maiden name. My Dad's full name is Landrum Allen Fowler. He goes by "Allen," but Landrum was his grandfather's name. Back when I was born, doctors didn't know if you were coming into this world as a girl or a boy. If I were a boy, my parents planned to name me "Landrum Allen Fowler, Jr.," and call me "Landy." Thank God I was a girl.

LEAVIN' IN A BLAZE OF GLORY

Now let me be clear, we Southerners savor saying goodbye just as much as we savor saying hey. And we can say it in ways that require interpretation. "I gotta light a rag" and "I gotta go see a man about a dog" both mean "It's time for me to go." And like our greetings, Southern goodbyes are seemingly endless. A guest will say, "Well, I reckon I better mosey." The host replies, "Well, I wish you didn't have to rush off." Then the guest and host proceed to talk for another fifteen minutes. The guest then remembers, "Honey, I really gotta go." So the host hugs the guest and walks them outside saying, "It was so good seeing you, hun. When am I gonna get to see you again?" The guest replies, "Lord, I don't know, my kids keep me busier than a moth in a mitten. Oh, I forgot to tell you that I ran into our old piano teacher at the nursing home. She said to tell you heeeeey." The host responds, "Lord, I never practiced. That woman musta hated me. How is Mrs. Clary doing these days?" The guest gets into her car and rolls down the window so they can proceed to talk about Mrs. Clary for another ten minutes. Finally, the guest will crank up the car and drive off hollering, "Bye! Tell your husband I hate I missed him!" The host waves and hollers back, "I'll tell him if he ever gets off the dadblame golf course! Bye! Be careful you don't get sirened down!"

Southerners also make a big hooptydoo out of saying goodbye to the deceased. We go out of this world in a big blaze of traditional Southern funeral glory. But no one "dies" in the South. They "pass on," or they "take a call from Jesus," which can be signified by a large glitter telephone embedded in a gigantic casket floral arrangement that says, "Jesus called." We have some distinct funeral traditions and protocols you're not likely to find in other parts of the country.

First, there's the food. Southerners believe wholeheartedly that the only thing that alleviates grief is food. The minute news of a death spreads, an avalanche of food arrives at your doorstep—usually in the form of a casserole. Every Southern woman has a go-to death casserole recipe. I call these *disasteroles*. These are always homemade, freezer-friendly, and arrive in a dish with a lady's name written on the underside—'cause once the body's underground, she's gonna need her CorningWare back, hun.

Funeral food can vary in different Southern regions. My Virginia friends tell me ham biscuits are a funeral must, and my Mississippi friends tell me it's bad luck to bury a body in the Delta without eating tomato aspic. No matter what Southern state you're in, one thing is for certain: there will be deviled eggs. It's hard to be upset when you're eating a deviled egg.

Cremation is not as popular in the South's Bible Belt as it is in other parts of the country. I reckon that's because folks have spent their entire lives in fear of hell's fiery fury, so they don't want to risk that kind of double jeopardy. Instead, folks pay a small fortune to be buried in a cemetery and often those plots were purchased many, many years in advance of death because Southerners are peculiar about who they keep company with, even in death. Southern funeral protocol usually dictates that the deceased's family "receives friends" at the funeral home or family home, which is filled with grand floral displays. A camellia-scented room is most appreciated by those waiting in a long line to view a dead body.

When my Papa Fowler died, my husband, a New Yorker, attended his first Southern funeral. As we approached Papa's casket, my hubby nearly fainted when he realized it was open casket. As he struggled to keep his knees from buckling, I wept and repeated, "Papa looks good, dudn't he? Dudn't he

Southerners are peculiar about who they keep company with, even in death.

look good?" I needed reassuring, because Southerners like to go out of this world looking their best. Death is no excuse for not being well put together. Southerners select their casket outfits and discuss their death hairdo with their beauticians long before they die. When mourning a loved one, you never want to hear, "He hated that tan suit," or "They didn't fix her hair right," or "She'd die all over again if she knew she was laid out on display in that awful shade of coral lipstick."

> **Death is no excuse for not being well put together.**

After the bereaved receive friends, the grand florals are moved to the funeral service itself, which is usually in a church and most always a public affair. The attire is black and conservative, and there's lots of music, tears, and "amens," followed by a passionate sermon designed by the preacher to get your butt in church more often by reminding you of your own inevitable death. After the funeral comes the slow processional to the graveyard led by a police car and the hearse. Processionals are highly respected in the South, so cars pull over to allow the processional to pass. This is Southern courtesy at its finest. And in New Orleans, when a prominent figure dies, second processionals known as "second lines" form. The community grabs their brass instruments, playing lively tunes like "When the Saints Go Marching In" while following the hearse to the cemetery.

The fact is, we Southerners don't know how to say bye quickly or demurely. If you need some entertainment, I highly recommend reading the lengthy and often colorful obituaries in a Southern newspaper. I hope my loved ones write me a long, comedic obituary, because my favorite sound is laughter. And I'd like to be buried in a Kelly green dress with tasteful gold jewelry. And please, make sure my hair is red and not gray. And I'd like it blown out straight and parted on the left side so it looks "classy" like my Mama prefers it. When I meet Mama in the afterlife, I do not want her first words to be, "Sweetie, that middle part is not flattering to your face."

Alright, I gotta run so I can get busy writing another essay. But before I go, remember that I require an ivory shade of foundation. I'll be truly humiliated if I'm forced to say goodbye to this world with a face the color of a Clemson tiger. That's my definition of hell. Okay, now I really gotta go. Oh, but I can't forget to tell you that I look best in blush and lipstick that do not have any blue undertones. Oh, and I'm not picky about flowers but I despise baby's breath. Baby's breath better not come within five hundred feet of my casket. And I want live bluegrass music at my funeral so everyone can dance and celebrate my Southern. Okay, that's all for now. I'm really goin'. For real. Bye y'all! Smooches, pooches, poodles, and toodles!

Howdy y'all!

Howdy Do!

Hey Honeydrops!

Hey Shug!

Hey Sugarbooger!

Hey Sweetness!

Hey Sweetie Pie!

Hey Honeybun!

Hey Honey Bunny!

We've howlied but we
haven't shook.

I haven't seen you in a month of Sundays!

How's your
Mama and 'nem?

Well, look at you
lookin' like you look!

I'm so excited to see you I'm
walking pigeon toed!

Jolly boy howdy,
I'm happy to see you!

Well, aren't you
a sight for sore eyes!

I've been
chompin' at the bit
to see you!

Fancy seein' you here!

I haven't seen you since you
were wet behind the ears!

Hey y'all,
sit down for a spell!

Put your sittin' britches on!

Let's chaw the rag!

How is every little thing?

I'm just hunky dory,
how you doin'?

I'm fine as peach fuzz!

I'm finer than a frog's hair!

I'm fair to middlin'.

I'm still on the right side of the dirt.

I got one wheel down and my axle's draggin'.

I'm happier than a bed bug in satin sheets!

I'm happier than a goat eatin' sawbriars!

I'm happier than
a tick on a hound dog!

I'm busier than a three-legged cat
tryin' to cover it up!

I'm busier than
a funeral fan in July!

I'm busier than
a blind dog on a gut wagon!

I don't know her from
Adam's house cat.

She's as welcome as
an outhouse breeze.

He's as welcome as a
porcupine at a nudist colony.

She's 'bout to spit out a baby.

She's got one in the chute.

Good Lord, she's storked again.

Granny went
to meet her maker.

That's the prettiest corpse I've ever seen.

He looks real
natural, doesn't he?

Good gussie, her casket makeup looks like death.

Guess I'd better
skedaddle on outta here.

I gotta head for the barn.

I'm off like a dirty shirt!

It's time to put
the chairs in the wagon.

I gotta cut a trail.

Let me get back
to my rat killin'.

That 'bout puts the
rag on the bush.

I'll get up with ya later.

Y'all come back now, ya hear!

Bye, if ya need anything
just holler at me!

Embrace the Dadblame Weather

The Dadblame Weather

"We're fixin' to get a frog strangler."

THERE ARE SOME FOLKS YOU JUST CAN'T TRUST in life. Mother Nature is one of 'em. Do not trust her any farther than you can throw her. She's slicker than a pocket full of puddin'! You just never know what this crazy woman's gonna do, especially in the South. Ice storm in April, hurricane in May, July 4th tornado, 70 degree Christmas—I'm tellin' ya, she's crazier than a sack full of house cats! Her only predictable quality is her unpredictability. But if you live in the South, you must learn to embrace Mother Nature the same way you learn to embrace a difficult mother-in-law: with fear and respect—and plenty of wine. The South has always had extreme weather, and as global temperatures rise, the weather is only getting more erratic. But because we're prideful people, Southerners have long considered it a badge of honor to be able to withstand such inhumane conditions.

HURRICANES

As I'm writing this essay, tropical storm Barry is moving through the Gulf and is expected to hit southeast Louisiana and southwest Mississippi. The National Hurricane Center is predicting twenty inches of rain and a life-threatening storm surge. My dear friend Delaine is from Louisiana, so I started texting and calling her early this morning, as I am worried about her and her family. Hours later, Delaine *finally* sent me a text: "Sorry I couldn't pick up the phone earlier, darlin'. I'm at a hurricane party. Can't talk. Too loud." Then she texted me a picture from the party. Looked like a picture from a Mardi Gras party—full of toothy grins and booze.

Now, don't get me wrong. Louisianans fully understand the danger. They make preparations. They are old pros at hurricanes. But when they don't feel the threat is high enough to evacuate, the only reasonable thing to do is throw a neighborhood hurricane party and whip out the fine china and crystal. Hurricane-force winds are no excuse for inelegance. Obviously, hurricanes are extremely tragic, but a Southerner's reaction to a hurricane can be so funny that I actually made an entire YouTube video on the subject called *Sh%t Southern Women Say In A Hurricane.*

If you live in the coastal South, hurricanes are simply a way of life. You take the risk and become skillful at preparing so you can live in a place that speaks to your soul like no other place on earth. Folks in California make the same trade-off living in earthquake country. They trade in their fear for the gorgeous year-round weather that defines Southern California. I reluctantly moved to Los Angeles due to my husband's career and wasn't initially concerned about earthquakes. Then I felt my first one. It scared the bejesus outta me. I didn't know whether to scratch my watch or wind my butt. I am now well-versed in earthquake protocol, but this has done absolutely nothing to mitigate my earthquake anxiety. My Southern nature is accustomed to predictable forces of nature, like hurricanes and tornadoes and two inches of snow. Forces one can prepare for. Let's just say my prayers now regularly include, "Dear Lord, please don't let me die in an earthquake . . . or sitting on the toilet."

WEATHER IN THE SOUTH

Another thing I can't get used to in Southern California is the lack of seasons. In Los Angeles, we have summer, summer, summer, and summer. In the South, we have winter, pollen, summer, and football. And even though the seasons in the South are as unreliable as a politician's promise, I still miss 'em. Especially the fashion that accompanies Southern seasons. Hotter than the hinges of hell? Then, sweetie, you must wear seersucker and keep a church fan in your pocketbook. Headed to church on Easter Sunday? You must break out a wide-brimmed sun hat and floral dress, even if it's raining pitchforks and plows. Attending the homecoming football game? You gotta throw on several layers of perfectly coordinated school colors so your outfit is as versatile as fall temperatures. Going to Mee Maw's for Christmas dinner? You're obligated to wear a Christmas sweater, even if there's a warm front and you're sweating worse than the turkey did prior to landing on your plate. I'm convinced the South's unpredictable weather is the reason Southerners insist on changing their decorative wreaths each season. Some days it would be impossible to know you're smack dab in the middle of spring without that robin's egg wreath hanging on your front door.

SPRING

Southern springs are defined by pollen. Nonstop pollen. This is supposed to begin in March, but often creeps in as early as February. Southerners sneeze and cough and pray for rain to come and wash it all away. But *if* the rain ever comes, it usually arrives in the form of hailstorms or thunderstorms. Hail the size of baseballs that'll jerk tears from your eyes as you helplessly watch it destroy your brand-spanking-new pickup truck. Thunderstorms louder than a freight train and laced with lightning that crackles so fiercely you find yourself shaking worse than a hound dog trying to pass a peach pit. And just in case you're not terrified enough, spring also marks the beginning of tornado season. That means Southerners get to spend some quality time sitting in school hallways with text books over their heads, sleeping in their basements, or sitting in their closets for so long they find themselves wondering why on earth they insist on keeping clothes that haven't fit them since Jesus was a baby.

SUMMER

Then, of course, is the most famous of seasons—summertime in the South. The heat index often hits triple digits. You can bake biscuits in your mailbox. But the heat is friendly as a missionary compared to the unrelenting humidity. Southern humidity is B-R-U-T-A-L. It's more oppressive than a dictator. The air's so thick you can slice it like loaf bread. A Southerner's most important summer accessory is air conditioning. However, if a Southern woman finds herself in a

The heat is friendly as a missionary compared to the unrelenting humidity.

social situation without it, she takes pride in being able to gracefully withstand the heat. Horses sweat, Southern ladies *glow*.

Southern summers also bring more ferocious thunderstorms as well as hurricane season, which is certain to force you and your family to flee your long-anticipated Myrtle Beach vacation and shove you right into the last tee-niny motel room available in Gatlinburg, Tennessee. And, of course, with hurricanes come floods. Devastating floods. And more water only makes the South's mosquito problem worse. Summertime skeeters are big as house cats and stubborn as mules. Hollywood oughtta make a horror movie about gigantic mosquitoes that devour the entire Southern population called *Psycho Summer Skeeters*! I smell a blockbuster.

FALL

If the South is lucky, then fall brings beautiful football weather. Not too hot. Not too cold. And the foliage turns into a spectacular canvas of autumn color. There is simply nothing more breathtaking than a proper Southern fall, especially in the mountains. But fall tends to run about as smoothly as your great grandpa's antique weed eater. Fall flirts with the South, but then summer gets all jealous and shows up again like, "I know y'all missed me so I'm back to love y'all up with a romantic 92-degree humid Saturday." Plus, those pesky hurricanes are a threat until November. *And* the second tornado season begins in November. *And* we also get the privilege of a second pollen season, which lasts through November. And sometimes the crisp, cool fall weather skips the South all together and just snaps right into winter, which the South is the least prepared to handle.

WINTER

Winter gives Southerners a full-fledged nervous breakdown. Cold weather is rude, y'all. Real rude. And Southerners have no tolerance for such rudeness. Our favorite parts of winter are Christmas Eve, Christmas Day, and watching our Northern friends struggle to dig out of winter on the news. You see, snow makes Southerners pitch hissy fits. Hissy fits with tails on 'em. Before the snow arrives, we run like maniacs to grocery stores and wipe the shelves clean of milk and bread. We're convinced the blizzard will be so massive we won't be able to get to the grocery store again until March, so we fully prepare ourselves to survive for months on milk sandwiches. Every dadgum thing in town shuts down, which throws everybody into a tizzy except Southern children, who are happier than a pig in mud they don't have to go to school.

Then we watch in awe as the snow begins to fall. It's so beautiful, so peaceful, so Christmas! But after an eighth of an inch dusts the yard, it usually stops accumulating. But it keeps falling for hours, making the ground wetter and wetter. Soon the roads ice over. Then the power lines ice

Cold weather is rude, y'all. Real rude.

over. The ice lasts for days, bursting pipes, shutting off electricity, and generally wreaking havoc on the community. Soon Southern parents find themselves stir-crazy—sipping hot toddies, munching on bread, and trying to convince their kids that there's plenty enough snow to go outside and play in. I can't tell you how many "snow days" I spent as a child trying to sled on wet dirt. I made a lot of snowmen that looked downright anorexic.

I never realized what a winter wuss I actually was until I lived in New York City. It was the month of July when I first moved to NYC to pursue my dream of performing on Broadway. I laughed at New Yorkers as they whined about the summer heat. Weaklings! But as October arrived it got chilly and I realized I needed to purchase a warmer coat. Then November arrived and I realized I had to purchase an even warmer coat. Then December arrived and I realized I needed to purchase an entire new wardrobe suitable for exploring the North Pole. New York is a city filled with tall buildings, which turn every street into a wind tunnel. And it's a walking city, so one has to waddle through the streets of Manhattan like a dern penguin, fighting bone-chilling wind, ice-covered streets, and forty-eleven inches of filthy black slush and snow. I was not amused.

I remember waking up one morning to my first New York snow. Al Roker said the city was going to get a foot of snow. Do what? A foot?!? I ran to the store and stocked up on food and was fascinated that the shelves were still fully stocked with milk and bread. When I got back to my apartment, my agent called and berated me for not showing up to an audition. I said, "I'm sorry, I assumed it was canceled due to the snowstorm." She screamed, "Listen, Scarlett O'Hara, unless the entire island of Manhattan falls into the Hudson River, nothing is ever canceled!" Over the course of my many winters in New York, I found myself performing in the cold, pouring rain during the Macy's Thanksgiving Day Parade, performing on the *Today Show* in freezing winter weather on the covered ice rink at Rockefeller Center, and regularly arriving at the theater two hours before curtain so I had ample time to defrost and warm up prior to performing a Broadway show.

WEATHER SUPERSTITIONS

During my New York years, I waited with bated breath to hear the first thunder during spring, because Southerners believe that's a sign winter has broken. (Turns out, this superstition does not apply up North, where winter punishes until May.) In any case, Southerners subscribe to many superstitions about the weather. If a rooster crows at eight o'clock at night, he'll wake up with a wet head. If the trees are full of nuts and the squirrels have real bushy tails, then it's going to be a bad winter. If chickens come out and eat during a rainy day, then you're in for a major rainstorm. If there's lightning in the winter, it'll snow within a week. If there are circles around the moon, it's gonna rain. And if you need rain, hang a dead snake in a tree and it'll rain within the week. Perhaps the most famous of these superstitions is that if it rains on your wedding day, your marriage will be full of tears. My wedding day was beautiful, and my marriage is full of love and laughter. But if my Yankee husband ever suggests we move back to New York and deal with those winters again, then I'm gonna cloud up and rain all over his ass!

It's fixin' to
clabber up and squirt.

*It's raining harder
than a cow pissing
on a flat rock.*

Looks like we're
gonna have a toad floater.

It's comin' up a gully washer!

It's hotter than Atlanta asphalt in July.

It's so hot the hens are laying hard-boiled eggs.

It's hot as foo diddly!

I'm sweating like a whore in church.

It's hot as blue blazes.

It's hotter than two squirrels wrestling in a wool sock.

It's hotter than a hooker's doorknob on payday.

It's hotter than a pot of collards!

It's hotter than a burnt clutch!

It's hotter than fried hell.

It's hotter than the devil's toenails.

It's hotter than a June bride in a feather bed.

It's hotter than a billy
goat's butt in a pepper patch!

It's so hot
the fish are sweatin'.

It's colder than an ex-wife's heart.

It's colder than a banker's
heart on foreclosure day.

It's colder than
a well digger's knees.

It's colder than
a cast-iron commode.

It's colder than
a whore house on strike.

It's colder than a
witch's tit in a brass bra.

The roads are slick
as an onion peel.

The roads are slicker than owl poop.

The roads are slicker than hen splat on a pump handle.

The roads are slicker than snot on a baby's lip.

It's drier than a popcorn fart.

It's drier than happy hour at the Betty Ford clinic.

It's so dry the trees are bribing the dogs.

It's so dry I'm spittin' cotton.

It's so dry the catfish
are carrying canteens.

The wind's gonna blow up a
gust of woodpeckers.

That tornado
'bout blew my drawers off.

The wind's blowing harder
than a hooker at a truck stop!

Tornadoes are like love: they sweep you off your feet and sometimes take your house.

Good Lord willin' and the creek don't rise.

Water's high, let's fish off the porch.

This hurricane is moving slower than a drunk snail.

Thank God it's a hurricane and not snow!

Waiting on the river
to crest is like
being stalked by a turtle.

Do pearls go with waders?

Have you seen my
monogrammed duck boots?

If the sun's shining while
it's raining, the devil is
beating his wife.

If wind blows smoke
down the chimney,
it's gonna be a bad winter.

**If the cows are laying down,
it's gonna rain.**

Sugar, if you don't like the
weather, just wait a minute.

Embrace
Your
Obsession
with
Football

Your Obsession with Football

"That wide receiver runs like his feet are on fire and his butt is a-catchin'!"

SOUTHERNERS LOVE SPORTS more than a skeeter loves a blood bank. I reckon we're just competitive by nature. NASCAR, wrestling, baseball, softball, tennis, golf, horse racing, and basketball are all popular in the South and are participated in and followed with ferocious passion. And while hockey and soccer have not been historically popular in the South, both sports have recently gained momentum and fans in the region. Hunting and fishing are not merely pastimes. They are cutthroat sports that require rising at ungodly hours in hopes of landing a tournament trophy. Or maybe just a living-room-wall trophy. Looking for a steady Southern career? Try taxidermy. But there is one sport steeped in Southern tradition more than any other. One sport that's woven thicker than a Bojangles' biscuit into the fiber of Southern culture. One sport that is considered the holy grail of Southern sports—FOOTBALL, Y'ALL!

In the South, football is a religion. It's gospel. And if you have not been baptized into the almighty football faith, then all we Southerners can do is pray for your wretched soul. Never tell a Southerner "I don't watch football" unless you want them to think some of the cheese has slid off your cracker. A Southern football fan might not remember his wedding anniversary, but he remembers exactly how many interceptions the Tennessee quarterback threw in the 1981 Tennessee vs. Kentucky game. Southern women know their football, as well. Northern fathers expect their daughters to understand Sylvia Plath. Southern fathers expect their daughters to understand pass interference. Football is etched into a Southerner's DNA. Those *23andMe* folks need to figure out how to include this in their genetic results, 'cause I'm certain proof of the Southern football gene would plumb stun scientists around the world.

So why are Southern culture and football so intertwined? First of all, let me clear one thing up: our obsession is with *high school* and *college* football. We might have a favorite NFL team, but we treat 'em like a redheaded stepchild. We just don't care as much for professional football.

Southerners are chained to their history, so of course our football obsession traces back to the Civil War. After the Civil War and Reconstruction, the South was dominated by the financially and industrially stronger regions of the North. Feeling an overwhelming sense of defeat on their own land, Southerners' spirits were lower than a snake's belly and the South was reckoning with its poor reputation due to the Civil War. Even Southern universities were considered much less prestigious than Northern universities. But this all changed in 1926, when the University of Alabama football team won the Rose Bowl and the National Championship against the University of Washington. This distinguished accomplishment on a national stage ignited a fire of pride and football gloating that still roars throughout the South today.

Even so, for years and years, the Southern region had very few professional teams and the few ones we had were located in major urban cities. Most of the population lived in the rural South, so the only choice was to invest in a local high school or college team. Even today, with the addition of several NFL teams in the South, the prevailing Southern opinion is that college football is just a lot more dadgum interesting than professional football. Why? It's simple. Professional football is a copycat sport. Coaches copy the offense and defense plays of other teams until they stop being effective because everyone else in the NFL is doing it. In college, each coach has his own idea of how the defense or offense will be run and a college coach is gonna run it that way even if it harelips the governor. This makes for a game wilder and more unpredictable than a rodeo bull.

If you want to watch a Southern woman lose all sense of ladylike decorum, attend a Southern football game.

FRIDAY NIGHT LIGHTS

Like most people raised in the South, my football education started early. My Granny Winnie was a quintessential Southern football fan. Fridays were reserved for high school football, and Saturdays were reserved for college football. My alma mater, Gaffney High School, has legendary football status in South Carolina, having won seventeen State Championship titles in the AAAA Division—which is tougher to do than sticking a needle in a lion's ass. Granny was an active member of the Gaffney High School Booster Club and, come hell or high water, she spent every fall Friday hollerin' at the high school game. If you want to watch a Southern woman lose all sense of ladylike decorum, attend a Southern football game. After each Friday night game, Granny would pick two or three players, whom she considered to be the MVPs of the game, and invite them to have dinner at her house the following Monday night. This was her ritual. When Granny died, we buried her wearing her beloved Gaffney High School football badges. Somewhere in heaven, she's screaming, "Come on Indians! Tear that quarterback's arm off and beat him with the bloody stump!"

My childhood is flooded with treasured memories of attending high school football games with Granny Winnie. We'd get all decked out in school colors, a fashion requirement, then Granny, nervous as a porcupine in a balloon factory, would smoke half a pack of cigarettes on the way to the game as we listened to local radio commentators make predictions and spew stats about the opposing team. She'd scream at the radio if she disagreed with the assessments and school me on why they didn't know crap from Crisco. As we fought for parking near the stadium, my belly would flutter with butterflies. I was in awe of the ginormous Gaffney High School stadium. The lights. The marching band. The cheerleaders. The electricity of a crowd so thick you couldn't stir 'em with a spoon. You see, up North, college football stadiums hold 15,000 people. Down South, *high school* football stadiums hold 15,000 people.

CHEERLEADING

As a little kid, I wished I could play Little League football like my cousin, Billy, who was a gifted player all the way to the college level. Billy flew outta the womb a big boy and he's a country boy with a fearless spirit, so Billy was a Little League football coach's wet dream. My Mama, of course, would have rather seen me go to juvie jail than see her baby girl play peewee football. So, I settled on being Billy's homecoming escort each year at his Little League homecoming game and playing football in the yard with Billy and his buddies. We played so hard my Mama had to sew double knee patches on my britches 'cause I kept tearing holes in them. I was the only girl. We played rough. I cried gator tears. Turns out, my skill set was much more suited for cheerleading than defensive lineman.

I was a cheerleader from seventh grade through my senior year, which carries bragging rights, because cheerleading tryouts are dog-eat-dog down South. That's a sport unto itself. We don't consider cheerleading antifeminist. We consider it an honor to spend a gajillion hours perfecting cheers, flips, and death-defying stunts. We consider it a privilege to sell program books, prepare elaborate pep rallies, and spend days painting museum worthy banners that the football team rips apart the minute they enter the field. We think it's fun to learn to draw our team logo on our face, painstakingly French braid our hair, and strut around the sidelines bare legged in thirty-degree weather. We eagerly wake up at dawn to wash forty-eleven cars and sell half a million Krispy Kreme doughnuts in order to purchase crisp new uniforms so we'll look cute as a button on the field as well as on a parade float. Why? Because we *love* football and take tremendous pride in displaying team spirit. We're quite proud of our manicured spirit fingers.

SATURDAYS DOWN SOUTH

Even though the high school football tradition of "Friday night lights" is a big fat deal, it's merely the opening act for the main event, which is college football—otherwise known as Saturdays Down South. Sundays might be for Jesus, but Saturdays are the real holy day. No right-minded Southerner would ever plan an event on a fall Saturday that conflicts with football. This includes funerals. And weddings. And births. That's because Saturdays are when the SEC, arguably the best conference in college football, waltzes out on stage and shows the rest of the country how football is done, huns.

Between the world-class marching bands, the live animal mascots, and the elaborate theatrics of introducing the home team onto the field, Southern college football games have more pageantry, pomp, and circumstance than the Miss America pageant. And our homecoming queens are also likely to be Miss America. So are our majorettes. Wanna see a gal twirl the daylights out of a baton? Attend an SEC game. There's also a lot of praying that goes on, followed by a lot of cussing: irony at its best. Scoring good

Sundays might be for Jesus, but Saturdays are the real holy day.

tickets is like winning the Mega Millions Lottery, as season tickets are passed down from generation to generation and fought over in divorce courts. Even the students enrolled in the actual college have to sign up for a weekly lottery to receive free tickets, because colleges rarely set aside enough stadium seats for the entire student body.

That's because Southern universities have fervent fans who are willing to spend big bucks for season tickets and travel expenses, and another small fortune on a coveted tailgate spot. You see, Southern tailgates are an event unto themselves. Fans arrive as early as forty-eight hours before the game to set up their tailgates, which include RVs, patio furniture, chandeliers, crystal, restaurant-grade grills and smokers, tons of Tupperware loaded with enough Southern delicacies to feed the United States Army, and enough beer, bourbon, and wine to quench the thirst of the entire college campus. And because tailgating is a major social event, we get gussied up. Men wear pressed khakis, oxford shirts, and hats with team logos. Women sashay around in school colors, creating a fashion show that rivals Paris Fashion Week, except with more sparkles.

Southern fans commit their souls to a college team whether they attended the school or not.

Ole Miss, as my Mississippi friend Kat loves to point out, has long been considered the best college football tailgate experience in the South. Her daddy, a former Ole Miss linebacker who played with Archie Manning, told me that Ole Miss fans share the philosophy, "Ole Miss might not win every game, but we ain't never lost a party." It's not uncommon to hear a Southerner admit, "I was havin' so much fun tailgating I never even made it to the game." And when the game is over, the tailgate continues. We keep celebrating if we win and if we lose, we tuck in our bottom lip, crack open another beer, and replay the game as arm-chair quarterbacks.

Funny thing is, Southern fans commit their souls to a college team whether they attended the school or not. Granny Winnie was a rabid Clemson fan, yet she never set foot in a Clemson classroom. When I received an academic scholarship to the University of South Carolina, I must admit I was glad Granny Winnie was already dead, 'cause it woulda killed her to watch me turn into a full-fledged cockadoodle-doo GAMECOCK! You see, in the South, college football rivalries are serious as a heart attack, and our rivalry isn't just reserved for football season. We trash talk each other all year long. Families must choose sides. Clemson or Carolina. Auburn or Alabama. Georgia or Georgia Tech. Such rivalries break up marriages. I remember the first time I brought my future husband home to meet my parents who were bumfuzzled by the fact that I was in love with a New Yorker. Daddy was seriously concerned but simply said, "Well . . . at least he's not a Clemson fan."

And perhaps that's what I love most about football: football has the ability to unite people from various racial, political, religious, cultur-al, and economic backgrounds. My Daddy and my hubby are polar opposites, culturally speaking, but football has been a glue that's bonded them over time as my husband, a Boston University graduate, adopted the University of South Carolina as his college team. Now he proudly wears his USC gear and watches the games with me on TV, as that is one of the few remedies for my homesickness. This is how I know my husband truly loves me. It's easier to put socks on a chicken than be a Gamecock fan. Nonetheless, we cheer them on from the West Coast. And I know Granny Winnie's blood is running through my veins, 'cause at the start of each USC game, this Southern lady loses all sense of decency and grace and crudely screams the USC cheer, "Y'all can't lick our Cocks!"

Did you get your clear regulated pocketbook for football season?

Is this dressy enough for tailgating?

I'm fixin' to plan my tailgate menu.

Honey, we got here two days before kickoff.

Where are y'all's seats?

Gettin' tickets was harder than
catching a cat in a whirlwind.

Darlin', can you
put another squirt of bourbon
in my Coke?

That fool planned a funeral
during football season.

I declare, I can see that
cheerleader's hootenanny.

Our homecoming queen
is finer than a new set of tires.

Those uniforms are tacky
beyond words.

That team's tougher
than a one-eared alley cat.

This new coach
is all hat and no cattle.

That touchdown was easier than
falling off a greasy log.

Y'all better stomp their livers out!

Rip through that defense
like Sherman through Atlanta!

Hit him so hard
his Granddaddy feels
it in his grave!

Bless his heart, he got
the living snot knocked outta him.

That linebacker's meaner
than an alligator in a drought.

That center's so tough he chews nails
and spits out barbed wire.

That running back is faster
than a chicken being chased by
Colonel Sanders.

He's faster than
a politician's promise.

He's slower than a constipated turtle.

He's slower than
a two-legged dog on Sunday!

That quarterback couldn't
drive a cat upstairs with a broom.

Our offensive line ate a whole box of stupid for breakfast.

If our defense was any lazier, they'd be in a coma.

Our kicker is useless as a football bat.

If we miss this field goal, I'm goin' back to tailgate.

Baby Jesus, please let us get the two-point conversion.

That quarterback couldn't hit the broad side of a barn.

Run the DAYUM ball!

If I had a cow as dumb
as that coach,
I wouldn't drink its milk.

Throw the DAYUM ball!

This game's
harder than bagging flies.

Catch the DAYUM ball!

Seems that ball's harder to catch then my husband's girlfriend.

I'm nervous as
a fly in a glue pot.

Anybody got a nerve pill?

Hey ref, you're
blind as a one-eyed bat!

Mercy sakes,
Coach is mad as all get out.

That ref is so crooked
he has to screw his socks on.

Coach ripped off
his headset quick as a rattler!

Mister Referee,
that dog won't hunt!

I'll be happier than a pup with
two tails if we just beat 'Bama.

I'll be dogged,
we can't win for losin'.

That coach couldn't teach a sittin' hen to cluck!

We're still wet behind the ears, we'll get 'em next year.

The preacher better not mention this game in church tomorrow.

I betcha hell has the Tiger Rag playing on loop.

We're gonna bury Paw Paw in an SEC-themed casket.

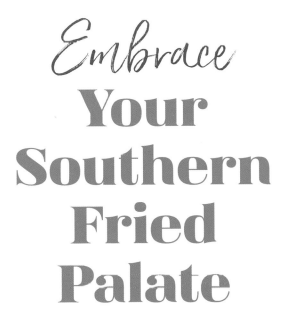

Embrace
Your
Southern
Fried
Palate

Your Southern Fried Palate

"Jeet yet?"

———

DOWN SOUTH, THE TEA IS SWEET but the server is even sweeter. That's because food is the ultimate form of Southern hospitality. New to the neighborhood? Somebody's gonna make you a peach pie. Christmas time? Somebody's gonna make you divinity candy. Your daddy just drop dead? The whole dadgum town's gonna bring you a casserole.

Eating is a form of art in the South. Southerners are offended by people who whine, "I'm not hungry." The only acceptable excuse for refusing food is that your jaw is wired shut. And even then, somebody's gonna take pity on your medical condition and bring you a freshly blended chicken and dumplin' shake to sip on.

Southerners show their deepest affection by feeding you fabulous, home-cooked meals from family recipes passed down through the generations. Where you are in the South determines what you eat. Sure, there are standard Southern recipes every Southern cook knows, but some foods are specific to Southern regions. If you're in the South Carolina low country, you'll find yourself slurping up she-crab soup. In Louisiana you're certain to chow down on jambalaya. Texans are likely to smother their chicken-fried steak in red-eye gravy while a Tennessean is likely to smother it in cream gravy. Every Southerner is convinced their way of preparing a classic Southern recipe is best. We're extremely judgmental about food. "Who made the tea?" is Southern for, "This tea is not fit to drink." We'll passionately argue for hours over how sweet tea should be or which state has the best BBQ but there's one thing all Southerners agree on—food equals love.

Based on this equation, I grew up with more love than one gal should ever receive. My entire Southern history rests on the tip of my tongue, because most of my memories are associated with food. Churning homemade ice cream reminds me of carefree summer days playing with my cousins in Uncle Jimmy and Aunt Linda's pool. Every single time I crack open a crab leg, I find myself telling the story of how, when I was as a child, my Uncle Larry taught me to expertly eat crab legs in Myrtle Beach. Thanks to Uncle Larry I can order crab legs in a fancy restaurant and eat them elegantly—a skill that never ceases to impress. And Uncle Larry always makes my grandparents' cornbread dressing recipe

The only acceptable excuse for refusing food is that your jaw is wired shut.

for Thanksgiving and Christmas, because this ensures that even though my grandparents have passed, they are always at our family holiday table. For me, food and family are inextricably intertwined.

My earliest memory of Southern cooking was watching Mama make biscuits. I was about four years old and I remember watching Mama make and roll out the dough and being excited that I got to help cut out the biscuits. Ain't no tellin' how many homemade biscuits I've eaten in my life. Some slathered in butter. Some slathered with home-made preserves. Some slathered with sausage gravy. I've also eaten about two tons of fried fatback. For all you non-Southerners, fatback is a cut of meat from a pig. It's literally the fat on the pig's back. Tra-ditionally it's used as seasoning, but I vividly remember sitting on the kitchen counter and discussing my day at school while Mama fried me up pieces of this Southern delicacy.

Funny thing is, Mama is a reluctant cook. She'd rather clean three hundred toilets than spend three hours in the kitchen. But Mama's greatest fear is being the subject of gossip, so she honed her cooking skills to ensure nobody would ever whisper, "Ewww, Claudia brought a store-bought pie." For the record, Mama makes a mean lemon meringue pie, a stop-you-in-your-tracks sweet tater casserole, and her macaroni and cheese is so good, it'll make your tongue leap outta your mouth and lick your eyebrow off your head.

Then there's my Daddy, who loves to eat more than rabbits love to procreate. One bite of pulled pork reminds me of countless child-hood trips with Daddy to his favorite BBQ joint in North Carolina. Like most Southern men, Daddy is a grill master and carries on a torrid love affair with his smoker. And he's always been a gardener, so he got me hooked early on mater sandwiches: white bread, garden tomatoes, salt and pepper, and plenty of Duke's Mayonnaise. Mayonnaise is a key ingredient in Southern cuisine, and noses will scrunch in disapproval if you make the crucial mistake of using a different brand. As a child, Daddy also got me hooked on banana sandwiches, which is simply banana, bread, and Duke's for days. He fed me fried livermush for breakfast and homemade cornbread with darn near everything. Pintos and cornbread, cabbage and cornbread, and his personal favorite—cornbread crumbled into a glass of buttermilk. Looking back, I now realize these were budget meals, but to me this was five-star dining.

Speaking of fine dining, I can't remember a holiday that did not include my Aunt Kathy's tater salad. My family always has covered dish holidays. Covered dish suppers are a big deal down South, and folks adhere to strict rules about who is allowed to bring what. You can't just volunteer to bring the tater salad unless a special election has taken place and your tater salad has been deemed the winner . . . by a landslide. Then you are fully expected to make tater salad for every covered dish occasion for the rest of your life unless you're laid up in the hospital. And even then, you'll be thrown plenty of Southern shade for making folks suffer through Ruby Mae's second-string tater salad 'cause it always has a *wang* to it.

In my family, Aunt Kathy is the tater salad queen. And it wouldn't be Easter without Aunt Kathy's famous "Big-Ass Ham." And yes, that's what we call it. Big. Ass. Ham. And she won't mind at all if you wash that down with some *adult juice*. After all, Jesus drank wine. Like many Southerners, my Aunt Kathy and I appreciate a good cocktail, but just so we're clear, Southern women never get drunk. We get *overserved*. Don't drink? Don't worry. The South serves plenty of *Baptist beer*. Ahem. I mean sherbet punch.

My granddaddy, a devout Baptist, musta notta liked sherbet punch, 'cause he grew muscadines and made his own wine. Papa Fowler and Granny Fowler always had a massive garden, and they are definitely the most responsible for developing my Southern palate and teaching me the importance of homegrown food. Southern cuisine is evolutionary in nature, influenced by African, English, Scottish, Irish, French, Spanish, and Native American cuisine. Regardless of the influence, Southern cuisine emerged from an agrarian society. New York and Los Angeles are filled with expensive restaurants touting award-winning chefs using organic, seasonal ingredients. But authentic Southern cuisine has always been a farm-to-table experience.

Granny and Papa Fowler were country cooks of the highest caliber. They pickled and canned everything except each other. Granny's fried chicken and fried okra were blue-ribbon worthy. And Granny served collards, black-eyed peas, and cornbread year 'round—not just on New Year's Day when it's traditionally served to ensure a prosperous new year. Papa Fowler kept

Truth be known, I owe my marriage to Papa Fowler's pecan pie.

several beehives and treated me to tastes of honey right out of the hive. As a child, I chomped on beeswax like it was Juicy Fruit gum. Papa and Granny taught me how to catch fish and I watched in awe as Papa cleaned 'em and Granny fried 'em up. It's downright shocking that there's still a fish left in Lake Greenwood. I thought for sure they'd all been fried up and dumped into a Fowler belly. And there's no shortage of Fowler bellies, because Granny and Papa were also sugar wizards. Blackberry cobbler, naner puddin', Christmas fruit cake, fudge, lemon pound cake, coconut layer cake, red velvet layer cake, Minnehaha layer cake, and more pies than you could shake a stick at. They had dueling pecan pie recipes, and each insisted theirs was the best. Truth be known, I owe my marriage to Papa Fowler's pecan pie.

You see, despite growing up eating like I was training to become a sumo wrestler, in actuality, I'd been training to become a professional dancer most of my life. Which is the only reason I was able to eat so decadently and not get fat as mud. I moved to New York City to pursue my dance career and along the way met a feller named Sam. He was born and raised in Manhattan. Bless him. I never expected to click with a New Yorker, but he was handsome and his personality was so infectious I invited him to come to South Carolina and meet my family for Christmas. Poor Sam had no idea what he was getting himself into. Granny and Papa Fowler were none too pleased that I was still single at the ripe old age of twenty-five and dating what I considered to be "artists" and they considered to be "hoodlums." They were convinced I was gonna wind up an old maid.

Sam, in total culture shock, was invited to my grandparents' house for Christmas dinner. This in and of itself was confusing because

Sam thought "dinner" meant supper. I had to explain that "dinner" is Southern for lunch. Supper is our last meal of the day. So, Sam found himself at my grandparents' dinner table—otherwise known as the interrogation room. You see, Southern food is a truth serum. Southerners use it to extract information out of new neighbors, new preachers, and suitors—especially Yankee suitors.

As Sam consumed his first home-cooked Southern meal, my family asked him a bazillion questions. Sam, under the influence of fried okra, which he'd never tasted before, blissfully obliged. He answered and ate and answered and ate and answered and ate. The more he ate, the more my family liked him. Sam didn't realize that his big appetite was far more impressive to my relatives than his fancy education. Papa Fowler had made the pecan pie and it tickled him to death that Sam went back for seconds and thirds. And Sam liked my Granny's Christmas fruitcake so much she gave him a tin of it to take back home to New York. I didn't fly back to New York with Sam because I had work to do in my dance studio in South Carolina, so later, Sam found himself alone and stranded at the airport due to a flight delay. The delay was so irritating he decided to console himself with a piece of fruitcake. He ate the entire tin of Granny's fruitcake before he ever boarded the plane.

Even though my family was initially unsure about my dating a New Yorker, Sam had already won them over. But I was nervous about having a serious boyfriend and wasn't itchin' to get married, so my family was certain I'd screw things up and run Sam off. So, Papa Fowler casually remarked, "You know that Sam really liked my pecan pie. I oughtta send him one." Then, quicker than a knife fight in a phone booth, Papa made a fresh pecan pie and FedExed it to Sam's office.

At the time, Sam was a television commercial producer working at a big advertising agency in midtown Manhattan. When the mail cart stopped at his office and delivered that pecan pie, his mouth flew open like a carp. He was so excited he called his coworkers into his office and shared it. Those Yankees didn't know what hit 'em. As Sam tells it, he was so overwhelmed by the amount of love and thoughtfulness contained in that pie that he decided right then and there he was gonna marry me. Papa Fowler knew exactly what he was doing by shipping that pie. He knew the way to a man's heart was through his stomach. So, here's an idea for all you single ladies out there using dating apps. Instead of posting pictures of yourself on your dating profile, try posting pictures of some lip-smackin' food made from your family's delectable recipes. However, living outside of the South has taught me that people don't consider *all* Southern food delectable. They don't understand our obsession with chains like Waffle House, Krispy Kreme, and Bojangles'. Lord knows I have a book's worth of memories from eating at each of these places. And many non-Southerners think some things Southerners eat

Southern food is a truth serum.

are downright weird. These fools don't know what they're missin'! Grits are proof God loves us. But if you make instant grits then you deserve to die a slow, miserable death. Fried green tomatoes are 'bout good as sex. Coleslaw isn't merely a side dish, honey, it's a hot dog condiment. And who needs a bread basket when you can have a basket of hush puppies.

Watermelon tastes better with salt. Boiled peanuts are manna from heaven. But if you've only got a bag of salted peanuts, then dump 'em in a long neck bottle of Co'Cola. If you're wonderin', "Co'Cola" means Coke. And all soft drinks in the South are referred to as Cokes. A slug of Coke is sure to help wash down some of the South's more interesting proteins like venison, rabbit, quail, gator, crawfish, squirrel, chitlens, and frog legs. Can't decide? Then eat turducken. That's a chicken stuffed into a duck stuffed into a turkey. Or frogmore stew. That's shrimp, sausage, taters, and corn all boiled up then dumped out onto a tablecloth of newspaper.

I once took a bottle of Cheerwine to a business meeting in Hollywood. Everyone was baffled because they thought I was rolling

If you make instant grits then you deserve to die a slow, miserable death.

into a meeting with an alcoholic beverage. And I've confused many New York and Los Angeles party hosts by asking, "Do you need me to bring any pickups?" "Pickups" is Southern for appetizers, and pickups are a food group all unto themselves. Pimento cheese is the South's caviar. Life is just better with pimento cheese. And if you're serving pickups, then you gotta have a cheeseball. It's sacrilegious to have a party without a cheeseball. Parties are also more excitin' with some sausage balls, cheese straws, finger sandwiches, country ham biscuits, fried pickles, bacon-wrapped dates, chicken and waffle sliders, congealed salad, and a hot dip. Doesn't matter what kind of hot dip as long as it contains more cheese than the state of Wisconsin. My personal favorite pickup is deviled eggs. Southern women can devil eggs 'til the cows come home. My Mama is no exception. She makes delicious deviled eggs and like most Southern women, she considers her deviled egg plate one of her most precious assets. Along with her massive collection of casserole dishes in every size and shape known to mankind.

I too have a plethora of casserole dishes, although my crumbled cracker-topped casserole cookin' recently hit a snafu. A couple of years ago, I started experiencing some serious health problems. It took six months and a slew of different doctors before the source of my health problems was discovered. I was diagnosed with a gluten allergy. As you can imagine, this was a devastating blow to my Southern fried palate. Gluttony is a sin, so I reckon God is punishing me for forty-something years of overindulgence. I cried like a baby in that doctor's office explaining that I couldn't possibly give up gluten because I would have to abandon so many Southern recipes that feed my soul. The doctor sternly pointed to my lab results and said, "You can give up gluten or you can spend the rest of your life covered in eczema and having explosive diarrhea." I gave up gluten.

It has been extremely challenging, but it turns out I didn't have to give up all the Southern recipes I adore. I'm slowly but surely learning to make some Southern cuisine gluten free. It's been a bumpy road, but I'm determined because Southern food comforts me. When I can't get home, I eat home. Each bite is wrapped in nostalgia. I whip out my cast-iron skillet and fry okra in pure cornmeal when I need to channel the sage wisdom of Granny Fowler. I make mater sandwiches on gluten-free bread when I'm missing my Daddy. Mama's "gluten-free" mac and cheese always soothes life's disappointments and reminds me I'm loved.

No one displays love through food quite like a Southerner. This is why my Mama never walks away from a big meal without making a plate for an elderly shut-in, or a sick neighbor, or a family member in the nursing home. I don't have children, so I pray one of you readers will take pity on me when I'm in the nursing home and bring me a plate of good Southern eatin'. I probably won't have any teeth by then, so make sure it's something I can manage, like naner puddin' with calf slobber stacked a mile high. And don't forget I'll need gluten-free 'nilla wafers. Come to think of it, I'll be in diapers by then, so that'll be my nurse's problem. Bring me the real deal!

Betcha all this talk about Southern comfort food has got ya hungry as all git out. So, I figured I'd share a few of my favorite recipes with y'all. The following pages contain a couple of my family's most treasured recipes—given with Mama and 'nem's blessing, of course.

Papa Fowler's Pecan Pie

Servings: 2 pies

½ cup sugar

1½ tablespoons cornstarch

4 large eggs

2 cups dark corn syrup

½ teaspoon vanilla

½ teaspoon salt

1½ cups chopped pecans plus whole pecans for topping pie

2 regular store-bought pie crusts

Preheat oven to 425 degrees. Mix together the sugar and cornstarch in a bowl. Beat eggs and stir them into the sugar mixture. Add corn syrup, vanilla, and salt to the sugar mixture and mix well. Spread chopped pecans in the bottom of two regular pie shells. Divide batter evenly between both shells. Top both pies with whole pecans. Bake for ten minutes at 425 degrees. Reduce heat to 325 degrees and cook for 40–50 minutes, depending on oven.

Note: *Papa Fowler worked hard and stayed busy, so he believed in saving time and using store-bought pie crust. However, if you prefer to make your own pie crust then go for it, huns!*

Granny Fowler's Pecan Pie

Servings: 1 pie

½ cup white sugar

1 cup packed brown sugar

1 tablespoon flour

2 eggs

¼ cup evaporated milk

1 teaspoon vanilla

½ cup butter, melted

1 cup chopped pecans plus whole pecans for topping pie

1 regular store-bought pie crust

Preheat oven to 375 degrees. Mix white sugar, brown sugar, and flour in a bowl. Beat two eggs and add to the sugar mixture. Add evaporated milk and vanilla to mixture. Add melted butter to mixture. Add chopped pecans to mixture and mix well. Pour mixture into pie crust. Arrange whole pecans on top of pie. Bake for 40–55 minutes, depending on oven.

Note: *Like Papa, Granny liked to save time by using store-bought pie crust. But Granny preferred to use brown sugar rather than corn syrup and she liked a stronger hint of vanilla in her pie. And Granny did not like to double her recipe, so she always made one pie at a time.*

Julia's Favorite Deviled Eggs

Servings: 12 deviled eggs

6 hard-cooked boiled eggs

¼ cup Duke's mayonnaise (Use another brand at your own risk)

1 teaspoon yellow mustard

1 teaspoon apple cider vinegar

2 tablespoons Mount Olive Sweet Relish (Squeeze out the extra juice from the relish)

Salt and pepper, to taste

Smoked paprika

To make hard-cooked boiled eggs: Place eggs in a single layer in a large saucepan. Do not stack eggs. Add enough cold water to cover eggs by at least one inch. Bring water to a rapid boil then remove the pot from heat, cover, and let it stand for 18 minutes. Drain hot water and replace with cold water and ice cubes. This ice bath will help you peel the eggs. Drain once eggs have cooled enough to handle. Peel them immediately. To peel a hard-cooked egg, gently tap it on the countertop, then roll it between the palms of your hands. Peel off the eggshell, starting at the large end.

For the deviled eggs, halve eggs lengthwise and remove yolks. Set whites aside. Place yolks in a small bowl and mash with a fork. Add mayonnaise, mustard, vinegar, and relish. Mix well. Season with salt and pepper to taste. Stuff egg whites with the yolk mixture, then sprinkle eggs with smoked paprika. Arrange eggs on deviled egg plate. Cover and chill until serving time (up to 24 hours).

Note: *My Mama uses relish and paprika, which give the recipe a daytime picnic kind of feel. For an elegant dinner party appetizer option, skip the relish and paprika, and instead garnish eggs with crumbled bacon, caviar, lump crab meat, or parsley.*

Aunt Kathy's Tater Salad

Servings: 6–8

1½ teaspoons salt

5 hard-cooked eggs

4 or 5 medium potatoes

1½ teaspoons celery seed

4 tablespoons Mt. Olive Sweet Salad Cubes

5 tablespoons Duke's mayonnaise

Salt and pepper, to taste

Paprika, for garnish

To make hard-cooked boiled eggs: See instructions on page 100.

For the Tater Salad: Put the potatoes in cold water with about 1 ½ teaspoons of salt and boil for about 20 minutes or until soft. Strain and cool completely. Peel the potatoes and cut into 1-inch cubes. Slice eggs. Mix potatoes, eggs, celery seed, Sweet Salad Cubes, and mayonnaise into a large bowl. Season with salt and pepper to taste. Arrange some egg slices on top and sprinkle the Tater Salad with paprika.

Note: *You can make this a day ahead; it'll "set up" real nice in the refrigerator overnight.*

Big Mama's Mac and Cheese

Servings: 6-8

1 (16-ounce) box macaroni

3 tablespoons butter

3 (7.5-ounce) packs of Sargento Chef Blends 4 State Cheddar Shredded Cheese, divided

3 eggs, beaten

2 cups evaporated milk

Salt and pepper, to taste

Preheat oven to 475 degrees. Bring a large pot of water to boil, then add macaroni. Boil about 10 minutes, then remove from stove and drain. Return macaroni to pot. Add butter and 2 ½ packs of cheese. Stir until butter and cheese are melted and blended. Add eggs, milk, salt, and pepper to taste, and stir well. Spray a 9 x 12 casserole dish with olive oil. Pour mixture into dish and sprinkle remaining cheese over top. Bake for about 12 minutes, but watch closely after 10 minutes, as ovens vary and you don't want it to burn.

Note: *This is so easy to make gluten free! Just use gluten-free macaroni and boil per the instructions on the box. Gluten-free pasta generally has a shorter cook time than regular pasta.*

Y'all come and git it!

Down South,
the dinner bell is always
in tune.

You can call me anything, but don't call me late for supper!

Jump on in
there and git ya some!

When in doubt, wrap it in bacon.

I'm so hungry I could eat
the butt off a hobby horse.

I'm so hungry I could eat
the paint off the walls.

I'm so hungry my belly
thinks my throat's been cut.

I'm hungry enough to eat
a dead skunk.

I'm so hungry my stomach's
lickin' my backbone.

I'm so hungry my belly's gonna sue my teeth.

I'm so hungry I could eat the south end of a northbound polecat.

Darlin', you eat like you've got a hollow leg.

That tastes so good it'll make a puppy pull a freight train!

This tastes so good it makes me wanna slap my mama!

That tastes so good my tongue slapped my brains out!

A cravin' for Chick-fil-A just flung up on me.

I've got a hankerin' for frogmore stew.

Down South, BBQ is a noun not a verb.

If I'd known you were coming I'd a fixed a cake!

Ewww . . . that tastes so bad
it'd make a buzzard puke.

I'm 'bout to bust a gut!

I'm full as a tick
on a ten-day suck.

Stick a fork in me, I'm done.

Always be aware when
you've had a gracious plenty.

You don't want people thinkin' you're the type of gal who uses instant grits.

There's a special place in hell for folks who make packet gravy.

She's so tacky she uses dark meat in her chicken salad.

That girl doesn't eat enough to keep a cat alive.

This wine is going down like honeymoon pajamas.

That'll put
a quiver in your liver.

He's drunk as Cooter
Brown!

Embrace
Your
Health

Your Health

"I'm so sick I'd have to get better just to die."

YEAR AFTER YEAR, Southern states consistently wind up at the bottom of the barrel when it comes to health and wellness. Seems downright unfair that the South's health continues to rank the lowest in the United States when Southern women are renowned for putting intense effort into their body's appearance. As I covered in *Talk Southern to Me*'s chapter on beauty and style, Southern women insist on looking well put together. We'll spend our last dime on bizarre beauty gadgets, face creams, cellulite tonics, teeth whiteners, lip plumpin' lipsticks, eyelash growin' mascara, fake nails, fake tans, fake colored hair, and "appropriate" outfits to flatter the bodies we exist in. And the grass is always greener: If we're short, we buy shoes to make us tall. If we've got curly hair, we buy straighteners. If our boobs are flat as a flitter, we buy push-up padded bras, and if we have big ol' whoppers, we buy reduction surgery. But it seems our efforts are misguided, because even though we work hard to make our bodies look good, study after study proves Southerners' bodies don't feel so good. Southerners live shorter, sicker lives and experience higher rates of cancer, diabetes, and heart disease. Well, hell's bells! No wonder we're always blessing each other's hearts.

So why do we Southerners tend to live shorter lives? One reason is the South has more unintentional injuries and accidental deaths than other parts of the country. A Southerner's famous last words are, "Hey, y'all, watch this!" Southerners are prone to attempt stunts on wheels, play with power tools, and fall out of tree stands. My cousin Billy broke both his arms attempting to replicate an Evel Knievel stunt on his bicycle. He was lucky he didn't break his neck. My cousin Brandon once tried to light a trail of gunpowder. That didn't turn out well. He was lucky he didn't blow himself to pieces. My Daddy accidentally shot himself while heading out to hunt. He was lucky his gun was pointing down and he only lost a toe. Funny thing is, after Daddy shot himself, the very first thing he said to his brother Jimmy was, "Don't tell Mama." That's 'cause Southern mamas will jerk a knot in your tail, scolding, "Have you lost your ever-lovin' mind?" at the exact same time they are forcing you to take a bath and put on clean clothes prior to taking you to the hospital. As a kid I broke my arm twice and busted my chin four times due to "Hey, y'all, watch this!" behavior, so I speak from personal experience when I say Southern mamas

A Southerner's famous last words are, "Hey, y'all, watch this!"

are determined to keep up appearances . . . even in the emergency room.

Another reason Southerners live shorter lives is because of unhealthy behaviors, such as smoking. Unfortunately, the South has more smokers than the rest of the country. Every Southern smoker I know genuinely desires to quit and would stand on their head for a solid week screaming, "I worship the New York Yankees!" if that was certain to cure their addiction. Too bad it's not that simple. Any smoker will tell you: kicking that habit is harder than nailing Jell-O to a tree. And of course, smoking cessation remedies can be expensive. In general, a Southerner's health can be greatly affected by economic challenges, which limit access to routine health care and expensive medicine. When you're struggling financially and busy working multiple jobs, you eat calorie-dense, processed food because, sadly, it's cheaper and faster than cooking fresh, unprocessed food. But even if you're so rich you buy a new boat every time your old one gets wet, you still live in a region famous for biscuits, BBQ, and baked layer cakes. A region where gravy is its own food group and the preferred cooking method is "fried to a crisp." We Southerners

We talk slow. we move slow. we eat slow.

also like to get our cocktail on. We especially have a taste for beer, Kentucky bourbon, and Tennessee whiskey, which are not exactly health tonics. But it's unfair to simply blame tasty Southern eatin' and drinkin' for the South's low health score. Yes, Southern cuisine is decadent, however most Southerners don't sit around eating fried food and layer cakes all day, every day. But we do sit around. A lot.

One of the biggest reasons Southerners tend to be unhealthier than the rest of the country is because we live more sedentary lives. The more sedentary we are, the more our butts spread out like potluck suppers—but it's often just too dang miserable to go outside and move around in the South's heat and humidity. Urban Southern cities like Atlanta have public transportation, which presents a daily opportunity to walk to the subway or bus stop, but much of the South is rural with little public transportation. This leads to lots of time sitting in a car, and too often folks are driving to a job or to school where they also sit for hours on end. And let's face it, even when we Southerners are up on our feet, we're rarely in a hurry. Southerners take their time. It's a way of life. We talk slow, we move slow, we eat slow. Even fast food is slow in the South.

Ironically, the South is full of fast athletes. Southerners are sports fanatics so it's common for Southerners to get lots of exercise playing sports in our youth. But as we grow older, we move off the field and into the stands, we get busy with our careers and families, and it becomes increasingly difficult to find time to exercise. I grew up dancing and during my years working as a professional dancer, I took for granted the fact that exercise was built into my workday. When I retired from dancing and began to pursue my writing career, I was downright shocked when my clothes began to mysteriously shrink.

Writing requires one to sit for long spells at the computer, which my Southern soul is well suited for due to years of training sitting on porches and chewin' the fat. But I refused to invest in a new wardrobe, so I got motivated to find a way to move more. In an effort to fit back into my favorite jeans and financially support my budding writing career, I became a certified apparatus Pilates instructor. But it turns out the job is to "talk" people through their workouts rather than work out with them. Now don't that beat a squirrel in a skirt! I put myself in a position where it was even harder to find time to exercise because I had to balance my workload of Pilates clients in addition to my writing projects. And now I'm a writer on the Netflix comedy, *Country Comfort*, where production provides us with an endless array of food due to the long workdays, plus I have an hour-long commute each way in LA traffic. Most days I'm so tired I'd rather recline in a dentist's chair and get a root canal than exercise.

So when my fellow Southerners tell me they want to be healthier, but it's difficult to find the time and discipline to do so, I truly empathize. Most Southerners are well aware they need to eat healthier and exercise more, but making lasting lifestyle changes requires a level of discipline that they'd rather reserve for more enjoyable activities, like quilt making, engine rebuilding, or reading the Bible cover to cover. Besides, it's so much easier to blame our health issues on genetics, isn't it? But the truth is, we aren't complete prisoners to our genetics. Dr. Oz explains it best when he says, "Your genetics load the gun, but your lifestyle pulls the trigger." The problem is that Southerners enjoy a darn good lifestyle, so it's nearly impossible to trade sweet tea for kale juice, fried taters for quinoa, and beer guzzling for bicycling. The common Southern philosophy is, "I'm gonna live my life doing what makes me happy. If that kills me, then please don't forget to keep flowers on my grave."

Even though the South is not a fitness-crazed culture, we are oddly fixated on talking about our bodies. Do not ask a Southerner about their health unless you've got nowhere to be for the next three days. Southerners are completely obsessed with discussing their myriad of health issues, array of prescription medicines and doctors, and the colorful details of their bodily functions. Spend time with a group of Southerners and you'll learn all about which heart surgeon you just gotta get in to see, which hospitals have nurses lazy as corn, how to find bargain cholesterol medicine online, how awful it is to be eat up with the gout, how aggravatin' it is to have the trots, how restless leg syndrome will drive ya bonkers, how impossible it is to sleep when your spouse has sleep apnea, how many youngins at school have the "strap" throat, how the humidity keeps ya galded, how compression stockings create a fashion crisis, and how you can always find ginormous pill box organizers on sale up at the Walmart. No matter how worn slap out Southerners are of their health problems, they never tire of talking about them.

Do not ask a Southerner about their health unless you've got nowhere to be for the next three days.

HOME REMEDIES

Such conversations inevitably lead to the discussion of Southern home remedies. Historically, Southerners living in the rural South had big families, and many did not have easy access to doctors or couldn't afford to see a doctor every time a child sneezed. Thus, they relied on home remedies. Folk medicine has a long history in the South, tracing back to Native Americans and the era of slavery. Native Americans have been practicing medicine for thousands of years, and many of their herbal remedies influenced Southern home remedies. African-American slaves were often denied access to Western medicine, so they relied on the folk medicine brought with them from Africa. This medicinal knowledge eventually filtered its way into white culture and became part of the Southern culture at large. Much of the African medicinal heritage has been preserved and can be found today in Gullah culture. For all you non-Southerners, Gullah people are African Americans who live in the Lowcountry Sea Islands and the coast of South Carolina, Georgia, and Florida, and are direct descendants of slaves from that same area. It's very likely that your

I reckon they don't teach Southern remedies at prestigious medical schools.

Southern grandma's famous home remedy for a stomachache has roots in either Native American or African culture. Regardless of the root, word of mouth is the quickest mode of transport in the South, and everybody is eager to share the home remedies that have been passed down in their family for generations.

My South Carolina friend Sheila tells me that no matter what the physical ailment, her mama always said, "You'll feel better if ya take ya a laxative." Instead of laxatives, my Granny Fowler treated everything except hurt feelings with red oil. My childhood babysitter treated the hiccups with a spoonful of honey. I don't know if it worked, because I faked the hiccups so I could get a taste of honey. What I do know works is turning completely upside down and swallowing water. My family always treated my bee stings with a wad of wet tobacco from a cigarette, and this always cured my childhood tears, because nicotine acts as an anesthetic. Mama always had a huge aloe plant and squeezed the plant's nectar on my sunburns—of which there were plenty. If I had a chest cold, my Granny Winnie would boil water, honey, ginger and lemons, and then add a shot of whiskey to the brew. Three years ago, I was misdiagnosed with bronchitis and survived three weeks on Granny Winnie's chest cold brew before landing in the emergency room, where I was diagnosed with whooping cough. The doctors were stupefied I withstood the violent coughing that long without the proper antibiotics. I reckon they don't teach Southern remedies at prestigious medical schools.

Ever had a chigger bite? For all you city slickers, chiggers are tiny larvae that live in weeds, grass, and wooded areas. They latch onto your skin and make themselves right at home. Although they are tee-niny creatures, these little suckers cause intense itching. My Daddy taught me to paint chigger bites with fingernail polish. You just paint the bite and that pesky chigger smothers and dies. Daddy also insisted that, to avoid ear infections and prevent wax buildup, it was important to boil out your ears regularly with peroxide. Daddy can barely hear himself hollerin', so let's not consider him an ear guru, but I can't recall the last time I had an ear infection. As a teen, I spot-treated pimples with toothpaste, but I've since discovered that tea tree oil works better. And I don't even remember who taught me that brushing your teeth with baking soda will whiten them and washing your hair with baking soda will remove product residue, but I've done both and gotten great results. I do remember one of my Sunday school teachers had the most beautiful fingernails; she told me to rub my cuticles nightly with olive oil and mine would grow long and strong as well. I clearly lacked discipline, because instead I wore acrylic nails from my teens through my early thirties. But it was olive oil that resurrected my natural nails after so many years of damaging the nail bed.

APPALACHIAN FOLK MEDICINE

My first cousin Angela is a brilliant nurse with decades of experience, but Angie's also a country gal who's been exposed to a treasure chest of Appalachian folk medicine. When Angie's daughter was a baby, she had a severe diaper rash. After following doctor's orders of no diapers, airing out the baby's butt, and using expensive steroid creams, the diaper rash was not one bit better. Angie was at her wit's end when her mother-in-law, Mrs. Martin (also a country gal), came to the rescue. She found a previously occupied dirt dauber's nest, ground it down to a fine powder and pressed it through cheesecloth. Then she covered the baby's butt with rosebud salve and sprinkled the powdered nest into the baby's diaper. Angie was astonished at how fast it worked. But if it hadn't, Mrs. Martin's next remedy was to soak the baby's butt in river water after it rained. If Angie's baby was agitated, Mrs. Martin calmed the baby with catnip tea, and she calmed the anxious parents down by boiling a mess of sassafras tea. Mrs. Martin treated sore throats by taking a tree branch, wrapping the end of it with Mercurochrome-soaked cotton balls, and then coating the back of the throat. She treated stomachaches with yellow root tea, and if you had a headache, she would put vinegar on a paper bag and tie it to your forehead. Mrs. Martin's cold remedy? Bake half an onion, squeeze the juice out of it, and drink it. Country people don't mind stinkin' to high heaven.

As a nurse, Angie of course relies mostly on Western medicine, but she swears by a few of her own home remedies. For chest colds she suggests using rock candy and moonshine, and she keeps gauze soaked in zinc oxide in her freezer to treat abrasions and burns. If you've got a "risin'," which is country speak for "boil," she suggests laying a piece of uncooked fatback on it. The salt from the pork draws out the impurities.

Country people don't mind stinkin' to high heaven.

Southerners don't *get* sick, we *take* sick.

And for general respiratory ailments, she suggests placing an onion and mustard poultice on your chest. Angie's come across many patients who swear WD40 improves their arthritis, but she believes it's the action of rubbing the skin itself that actually alters the behavior of nerve endings. And she strongly warns against using butter or mayonnaise for burns, as this never works and only creates infection. But I think my favorite home remedy tale from cousin Angie is about her grandmother, whom she called "Nanny." When Nanny was a child, she was being chased by a bull and ran into a barbed wire fence, which tore off half her ear. Rather than panic, young Nanny's mama mixed flour and water, created a paste, and set that ear right back in place. Stuff like this only happens in the South.

TAKING SICK

Lastly, I should point out that Southerners don't *get* sick, we *take* sick. And if you're gonna take sick, then the South is where you wanna be. Southerners are proficient in kindness and are trained to constantly think of others, so they truly go the extra mile to tend to the sick and elderly. Southern folks make it a priority to visit the sick, cook for the sick, send cards and flowers to the sick, call and check on the sick, and most importantly, pray for the sick. Whether you've been diagnosed with terminal cancer or an infected toenail, you're likely to find yourself on every church's prayer list in town.

At the end of the day, there's nothing more valuable than your health—'cept maybe your great grandma's chess pie recipe. And since we Southerners have many such decadent treasures in our recipe box, and are prone to rocking in a chair for hours on a porch, we're forced to work a little harder than the rest of the nation to stay healthy. But if we Southerners have enough discipline to trace our family trees slam back to Earth's creation, decorate our houses like a Christmas theme park each year, and spend fifteen hours prepping and roasting a whole hog, then surely we can channel some of that discipline toward our health. We must all keep in mind that even the smallest lifestyle changes can produce results. I wish all y'all good health and pray ya don't take sick anytime soon. But if ya do take sick, try to remember that ailments and happiness both increase the more you talk about 'em.

SOUTHERN REMEDIES

Abrasions: *Zinc Oxide-soaked gauze, red oil*

Age spots: *Apply buttermilk, rinse after 20 minutes*

Agitation: *Catnip tea*

Anxiety: *Sassafras tea*

Arthritis: *Red oil or emu oil*

Bee stings: *Tobacco*

Boils: *Raw fatback*

Burns: *Aloe plant, red oil, or Zinc Oxide-soaked gauze*

Chigger bites: *Fingernail polish*

Clean ear canals: *Hydrogen Peroxide*

Colds: *Boil water, honey, lemons, and fresh ginger; add whiskey to taste*

Bake half an onion and drink the juice

Rock candy and moonshine

Homemade chicken bone broth

Constipation: *Prunes*

Cuts and bruises: *Apply turmeric powder or red oil*

Diaper rash: *Previously occupied dirt dauber's nest ground down to fine powder*

Dry skin, lips, cuticles, nails: *Olive oil*

Earaches: *Place garlic clove in ear (do not shuck) or sweet oil*

Gout: *Eat cherries*

Hair product buildup: *Wash hair with a tablespoon of baking soda*

Hair conditioner: *Mayonnaise on the ends, then rinse well*

Headaches: *Ice or vinegar-soaked cloth*

Hemorrhoids: *Witch hazel*

Hiccups: *Spoonful of honey, or turn upside down and drink water*

Hypertension: *Eat garlic or drink diluted apple cider vinegar*

Indigestion: *Mix 1/2 teaspoon baking soda in water and drink*

Insomnia: *Lavender oil or lavender tea*

Joint pain: *Green tea, red oil, or emu oil*

Kidney stones: *Drink lemon juice daily*

Memory loss: *Sage leaf extract*

Nausea: *Ginger tea or ginger ale*

Nasal congestion: *Eucalyptus oil*

Puffy eyes: *Cold tea bags or cold cucumbers*

Razor burn: *Mashed avocados on skin*

Respiratory ailments: *Place an onion and mustard poultice on chest*

Ringworm: *Soak copper pennies in vinegar and apply solution to skin 2-3 times a day*

Skin ailments: *Colloidal oatmeal bath*

Sore throat: *Gargle with salt water*

Sore muscles: *Red oil, peppermint oil, or eucalyptus oil*

Stomachaches: *Yellow root tea*

Sty: *Drop of colloidal silver*

Toothaches: *Mix clove oil with olive oil and apply*

Urinary tract infections: *Cranberry juice*

Warts: *Cover with duct tape*

Whiten teeth: *Brush with baking soda*

Wounds: *Red oil*

Yeast infections: *Dead sea salt bath*

Zits: *Tea tree oil*

Disclaimer: I am <u>not</u> a trained physician, y'all. Please consult your doctor before trying any of these remedies for your ailments.

I'm usually fit as a fiddle.

My nose is
runnin' like a sugar tree.

I'm down in back again!

My knee's plumb swole up!

I feel like
death warmed over.

I'm so sick I need two beds.

I feel like death on a cracker.

I'm so sick and tired
of being sick and tired.

I feel like I've been drug
through the briar patch backwards.

I feel like I've been
chewed up and spit out.

I feel like I've been rode hard
and put up wet to dry.

I'm on death's door.

I'm sick as a dawg!

I feel like death
sittin' on a tombstone.

I feel more pitiful
than a three-legged dog.

I gotta tell the doctor 'bout my spells.

I've got the vapors!

He's eat up with lice.

I've got a
hitch in my gitalong.

Dern, I've jerked
a crick in my neck!

The best way to not
get pregnant is to hold
an aspirin between
your knees.

My legs have so many
varicose veins they look like a
Georgia road map.

I'm not fat, I just weigh heavy.

My doctor says I need a
rodeo clown to distract me at
the grocery store.

I think I'm overdrawn at
the memory bank.

If I had one more wrinkle,
I could screw my hat on.

Bein' old beats
bein' below the dirt.

Embrace
Bein'
Country

Bein' Country

"She lives way out yonder in my neck of the woods."

I'M OFTEN ASKED, "Which *Designing Woman* do you most identify with?" My ego wants to reply, "Julia Sugarbaker," because she's a
brilliant and feminine career woman who's not afraid to give a blister-
ing tongue lashing to any idiot who deserves it. But I'm not as whip
smart as her and my tirades aren't nearly as poised. My second instinct
is to answer, "Mary Jo Shively," because she's an artist and my redheaded spirit sister. But I've never had kids or been divorced and had
to reenter the dating world, so I can't relate to that part of Mary Jo. I
often want to answer, "Suzanne Sugarbaker," because she is a master
of men, loves to be the center of attention, and speaks her mind with
zero filter. Plus, I had the honor of meeting Delta Burke at a party in
Los Angeles, and she and I got on like two Southern peas in a pod. But
to be honest, I've never had Suzanne's level of vain confidence; I'm
much more measured with my words, and I've never had the luxury of
being rich. The truth is, even though I share qualities with the Southern
belles Julia, Mary Jo, and Suzanne, I mostly identify with Charlene
Frazier. Because, just like Charlene, I'm country come to town.

Country gals are different from pure Southern belles. Like Southern
belles, country gals know their manners, are kind and hospitable,
and can charm your socks off because they've been schooled in
social graces. But country gals are a unique paradox. The best way

to describe a country gal is half Southern belle, half redneck. As kids, they played with dolls, but they took their dolls to the creek to collect crawdads. They might not drive a truck, but they can. They sip mint juleps in Charleston but can whip out a keg stand in Panama City Beach. They can rock stilettos but prefer cowboy boots. They can navigate the country club *and* the hunting club. They ride parade floats and horses. They think George Clooney is handsome but lust for Jason Aldean. They have great work ethic because they weren't born with silver spoons in their mouths. They don't need a man to do everything for them because their daddies raised them better than that. And country gals aren't afraid to get dirty because, just like Wonder Woman, they can magically swirl up a polished look and go undercover as a pure lady. But country gals have to work twice as hard at being a lady. Seems like someone always finds a way to flip their redneck switch, and a country gal can go from lady to redneck in 2.5 seconds flat.

This is likely to happen if you call a country gal a "redneck." Don't do that. That's offensive, because the term "redneck" is historically derogatory, and it doesn't take into account the fact that there are varying degrees of redneck. There's *redneck lite, redneck prone,* and *full-fledged redneck.* Country gals might be redneck lite or redneck prone, but we aren't full-fledged rednecks. A country gal buys camouflage lingerie. A full-fledged redneck buys a camouflage wedding dress. A country gal can mow her own lawn. A full-fledged redneck drives her lawnmower to town 'cause her driver's license has been revoked. A country gal has a cousin named "Country." A full-fledged redneck has a cousin named "Booger Meth." Non-Southerners falsely make the assumption that all country folks are dumb, racist, trashy, full-fledged rednecks named Bubba and Bubbette. Nothing could be farther from the truth. Some of the smartest, kindest, most open-minded people I know are country folk. And they are a force to be reckoned with. As my North Carolina friend Clarinda puts it, there's nothing more dangerous than an educated redneck.

Ironically, country people are the *only* people allowed to refer to themselves as a redneck. And they may do so with pride. As in, "My redneck ass won the mechanical bull riding contest last night!" or "Aren't my new redneck wind chimes cute?" or "That fool kicked my dog, so I went full redneck on him." That's another thing. Country gals love animals. Southern belles have dogs and cats. Country gals have dogs, cats, miniature donkeys, chickens, horses, hedgehogs, fainting goats, rabbits, possums, and pet pigs. They'll go full-out redneck berserk if you mess with their animals. But even though we country gals have some redneck tendencies, we've got enough Southern belle training to mostly keep them tucked under our baseball caps. The biggest thing country gals like Charlene and myself have in common is that we're not ashamed of our humble backgrounds. We highly respect the country folks who raised us because we know they are responsible for making us who we are.

We're not ashamed of our humble backgrounds.

This sort of homegrown country pride is rampant in country music. Perfect examples include Jason Aldean's "She's Country," Blake Shelton's "I Lived It," Luke Bryan's "What Makes You Country," and Darius Rucker's "Homegrown Honey." Country music isn't simply about a sound, it's about celebrating the country lifestyle. A lifestyle that embraces family, positive values, and patriotism. Country music pays tribute to the working class, honors friendships, provides hope, and inspires country folks to get gussied up in their finest cowboy fashion—even if that's just a pair of worn-out Wranglers and a flannel shirt. My car radio is always tuned to country, and I chomp at the bit waiting for my annual girls' trip to Stagecoach, the nation's largest country music festival. And while I adore the music of pop country gals like Miranda Lambert and Carrie Underwood, my love affair with country music traces way back before they were born. In the words of current country darlin' Chris Young, "I was raised on country."

Just like Charlene, who idolized country music legends Jerry Lee Lewis, Mickey Gilley, and Johnny Cash, I too worship classic country music artists. My favorite television shows growing up were *Hee Haw* and *Barbara Mandrell and the Mandrell Sisters*. I totally relate to Barbara's declaration, "I was country when country wasn't cool." My Daddy was obsessed with singers such as George Strait, George Jones, and Conway Twitty, so classic country music provided the soundtrack to my childhood. We didn't have a lot of extra money for entertainment, so on Saturday nights we'd hang out at my Aunt Kathy and Uncle Larry's house because they were the only folks we knew who owned a big stereo equipped with a microphone. We were doin' country karaoke long before Americans even knew how to pronounce "karaoke." We'd belt out Loretta Lynn's "You're Lookin' at Country" and Conway Twitty's "Hello Darlin'" as if we were center stage at the Grand Ole Opry.

But my all-time favorite classic country artist is Dolly Parton. Dolly's the perfect personification of a country gal. She's a kind-hearted, well-mannered, Southern belle with a deep affection for big hair, bright sparkles, and bookoodles of makeup. But she also covets her hillbilly roots and has never tried to outrun them. Her extremely personal songs, "Coat of Many Colors" and "My Tennessee Mountain Home," are perfect illustrations. In fact, her entire business empire is a tribute to her modest childhood in rural Appalachia. And for all y'all non-country folk, that's pronounced "App-ah-latch-uh," *not* "App-ah-lay-cha." I'm from the Piedmont/Foothills region of South Carolina, which is a province of the larger Appalachian Mountains. Perhaps I've always gravitated toward Dolly because I also grew up hearing that specific Southern Appalachian accent. You'll hear an "-er" sound placed at the end of a word with a long "o." "Pillow" is pronounced "Piller." Words such as "Tire" and "Fire" are spit out as "Tar" and "Far." We use helping verbs, as in "I've done cleaned that." We use phrases like "pert near" instead of "pretty much near." And we ain't afraid to use the word "ain't," even though we're all schooled up and know better. Bottom line is, we sound like country bumpkins. But women like Dolly and my Mama have taught me that the most surefire way to disarm judgmental snobs is to completely own your country bumpkin status.

My Mama's parents never had much money, so her great-aunt Myrtle, who was wealthy and lived in Atlanta, offered to pay for Mama to go to college at Georgia Baptist College of Nursing. But Mama didn't want to run off to school in Georgia because she had fallen in love with my Daddy, who was raised blue-collar country on the "mill hill." Of course, Aunt Myrtle's ulterior motive was to pull Mama away from my Daddy in hopes that Mama would meet and marry a doctor and elevate herself from country gal to rich Southern belle status. Mama really wanted to go to college, but not in Georgia. She was in a pickle. Her financial solution? Enter a pageant! As a child, Mama had learned to clog at a bluegrass barn called Curley's Ranch and honed her skills clogging at weekend hoedowns at the local VFW. For youins that don't know, clogging is America's folk dance that originated in the hills of Appalachia. That being Mama's only talent, she clogged for her talent routine. To Mama's total shock, she was crowned Miss Cherokee County.

But being a country gal from such a small town, Mama was worried she was gonna stick out like a sore thumb at the Miss South Carolina Pageant amongst all the other highfalutin beauty queens from across the state. Those Southern belles had fancy clothes and classy talents like pointe ballet, classical piano, and opera. Aunt Myrtle, never one to be outdone, decided to finance Mama's interview dress and her evening gown in hopes of giving her an edge. But despite her two new outfits, Mama knew her best bet was to be exactly who she was, so she leaned into her authentic country soul. She waltzed

The most surefire way to disarm judgmental snobs is to completely own your country bumpkin status.

out onstage, wearing a cheap wig piece that would have made Dolly proud, and performed a comedic monologue poking fun of how country she was. Then, for her big finish, she clogged to the bluegrass tune "Twin Banjo Special." She even dragged two bales of hay out onto the stage to serve as her "props." Mama got a standing ovation. Nobody had ever seen anything like it. Mama was the first contestant to perform clogging as a talent in the Miss America Pageant system. Mama won the talent competition, and her mama was so excited she went directly to Cato's and bought Mama a dress off the rack just so Mama would have something new to wear for the opening parade of contestants during the final night of competition, which was televised. Mama was well aware that dress was the cheapest one onstage, but she wore it with pride, knowing her mama had made a financial sacrifice to buy it. Ultimately, Mama finished in the top ten, and received the college scholarship money she needed to attend Limestone College in her hometown. Now sugars, that there's how you embrace your country.

After Mama graduated college, she and Daddy got married and moved into a trailer

As soon as I could walk, Mama taught me to clog.

in rural Blacksburg, South Carolina. Soon, I was born. While other Southern belles' diapers were being changed in pink princess–themed nurseries, this country gal's nursery theme was good ol' trailer wood paneling. It was homey. As soon as I could walk, Mama taught me to clog. Instead of nursery rhymes, I was schooled on bluegrass music. Mama hauled me all over the Southeast to get instruction from the best cloggers she could find, including Simone Nichols Pace, whose daddy, Bill Nichols, is considered the grandfather of clogging. Soon, I was entering talent shows, clogging competitions, and kid pageants, performing my own comedic country monologues and clog dance routines. I literally followed in my Mama's footsteps. Here's a monologue I found:

> *Howdy!*
>
> *I'm just a little third grader at Central School.*
>
> *But everybody's tryin' to teach me the things influential people do.*
>
> *My Granny really worries about my culture these days,*
>
> *wantin' me to learn piano, voice, tap, and ballet.*
>
> *Good Lord! That woman wants me perfectly raised.*
>
> *I know that Bach and Beethoven are important to us all,*
>
> *but what's wrong with Lester Flatt? Earl Scruggs? And the "Wabash Cannonball"?*
>
> *I've got me a secret up in my head, ya see,*
>
> *I'm just a country girl and that's all I wanna be!*
>
> *So if y'all will sit back, relax, and don't tell my Granny what I've done,*
>
> *I'll get ta clogging, and we'll have us some fun!*

I was proud as punch to recite this, as well as forty-eleven other renditions my parents helped me write. But each monologue started the exact same way. I would enter the stage, doing my best Minnie Pearl impersonation as I hollered, "HOWDEEEEEEEE!" Perhaps now you truly grasp the level of my *Hee Haw* fandom. My monologues were clearly not Shakespearean quality, but funny enough, linguistic scholars surmise that the Southern Appalachian accent and grammar is a remnant of Elizabethan English. Well, I'll be a possum on a gumbush! City folks have been making fun of me my whole life for sayin' stuff like "might could" instead of "might be able to" and "like'ta" instead of "almost." I afeared I was ignorant, but turns out I was raised speakin' Shakespeare's tongue. All y'all city slickers can put that in your pipe and smoke it.

Speakin' of city slickers, I honestly didn't realize I was a country gal instead of a pure Southern belle until I went to the University of South Carolina in the big city of Columbia, South Carolina. This fact became crystal clear to me when I participated in sorority rush. Blueblood belles asked me questions like, "Now what does your Daddy do?" "Who are you wearing?" "Where did you summer?" I watched 'em clutch their pearls as I answered, "My Daddy works in a ball bearing factory and we're tickled he's finally workin' first shift. My friend Betty, who lives way out in the boonies and has a sewing trailer in her backyard, made my dress. Oh, and I *summered* in Lake Greenwood at my family's lake house. Ahem. I mean single-wide trailer."

Ultimately, I joined Chi Omega, whose members included plenty of pure Southern belles. But the Chi O belles were the type that were genuinely amused by my hillbilly tales, just as the Southern belles on *Designing Women* were always entertained by Charlene's country shenanigans. My sorority sisters were fascinated to learn that, as a child, I stored my marbles in the iconic *Crown Royal* purple bag; that gals from my neck of the woods considered goin' muddin', goin' to the dirt track races, or goin' to the tractor pull hot dates; and that my family invested in three different boats rather than a proper lake house. Who needs more rooms when you can float on a pontoon?

I taught both the preppy belles and the Yankee gals in my sorority that duct tape can fix anything except stupid. I taught 'em how to cop a clean squat when you have to pee so bad your eyeballs are floating and you have no other choice. I taught 'em to relish the taste of Vienna sausages when that's all you can afford—and I taught 'em to call them "little stand up wieners" instead of Vienna sausages 'cause it's just more fun to say. I taught 'em country wisdom, such as, "A crooked cornstalk can still have a straight ear," "It don't rain every time the pig squeals," and "You gotta choose if you want your life to be chicken or feathers." I even taught a few of them some basic clogging skills, because they were amazed that I spent weekends and

Duct tape can fix anything except stupid.

summers teaching clogging in my dance studio, traveling to clogging competitions, and clogging at theme parks, such as Dollywood, Opryland, and Carowinds.

All that dancing paid off as it eventually led me to a career in show business. But it also led me to New York and Los Angeles, where it has been constantly brought to my attention that I don't know how to give proper directions. It seems Southerners, especially country Southerners, don't give directions like other people. No matter how hard I try to explain where "yonder" is, non-Southerners can't seem to find it. I don't know why they get so perplexed. Southerners give very descriptive directions. We're clear as a bell. For example:

> *Tootie and Trigger? Yeah, I know 'em. They live way out yonder. It's 'bout ten miles or so as the crow flies. But I reckon you wanna drive on mostly paved roads so I'll tell ya how to get there. Keep on goin' down this road till ya pass old Duck Dobbins's house. Bless his heart, he ain't had a lick of landscapin' since his mama died. He's still low as a toad in a dry well. Anyhoo, you're gonna turn right, right there at Duck's house, and keep on goin' till ya hit that bridge down there near Grassy Pond, and then you gonna take ya first left and keep on a goin'. And be careful 'cause one time, slam outta nowhere, a deer ran out in front of me on that road in broad dang daylight and I nearly crashed in the gully tryin' not to hit him. Lord, it scared my mule! But anyhoo, you're gonna keep goin' down that road a long piece till ya see Beaver Dam Church sittin' up on the hill, and you're gonna take a right. Then you're gonna pass Salt Lick Road, Salt Creek Road, Old Salt Road, and then you're gonna go over the train tracks and now don't stop on the tracks, 'cause I*

heard on the news they've had to fire some train conduc-
tors for bein' higher than a Georgia pine. Just hurry on
over the tracks and go down that road till you go 'round
dead man's curve and don't rubberneck at all the crosses
on the side of the road where people have died 'cause
I'm tellin' ya, that curve's dern dangerous. Now here's the
tricky part. You'll come up on the Handi Hut, which'll be
on your right, right? You're gonna turn into their lot and
go 'round back till you see the gravel road that leads out
to a string of trailers. Go way on down that gravel road
till you see the trailer with that real pretty pit bull who's
always laid up on the concrete steps and take a left. If
you don't see the dog, then just look for the trailer with-
out any underpinning and take an immediate left. Trigger
and Tootie's house is all the way down at the end of that
road. You can't miss it, 'cause Trigger has an old-timey
truck sittin' up on cement blocks in the front yard. And
now don't you know that irks the snot outta Tootie 'cause
the inside of her house looks like something you'd see in
a magazine.

How on earth can these directions possibly be confusing? Beats
any GPS device I've ever used. I gaurandangtee fellow country gal
Charlene Frazier could follow these directions to Tootie and Trigger's
house. That's the thing about us country folks. Even if we wind up
livin' in a big city like Atlanta or Los Angeles, far away from the dirt
we were raised on, we still speak and understand "country." It's our
native tongue. I've dealt with people my whole life who assume I'm
dumb as a box of hair because I hold onto my country spirit, accent,
and grammar, but I've made it my artistic mission to celebrate my
down-home roots. Thank goodness I choose to celebrate my heritage,
because doing so led to the opportunity to meet my idol, the Queen
of Country, the one and only Dolly Parton herself.

I was shakin' like a leaf as I arrived to my first business meeting with Dolly. When she flung open her front door, the redneck in me like'ta died but the Southern belle in me somehow managed to smile, introduce myself, and firmly shake her hand. I wasn't sure how to chat with a living legend, but her accessible, kind, country demeanor put me at ease. I couldn't help but be flabbergasted by the fact that the same little country girl who spent her life idolizing Dolly and clogging her heart out at Dollywood now had Dolly's undivided attention. Don't that beat a hen a-scratchin'! Just like Charlene, Dolly has a huge heart and understands the importance of helping another Southern sister out. I'll forever be grateful to Dolly for bein' so supportive of my creative endeavors. But country gals like Charlene and myself are mostly grateful to Dolly for giving us a sense of pride and self-affirmation for who we are in the greater American culture. We country gals are a very special breed of Southern woman. We know not to get too big for our britches. We know better than to go puttin' on airs. We know that no matter where life takes us, we must *always* embrace our country.

They live so far in the woods, the blackbirds carry road maps.

They're so country they think a seven-course meal is a possum and a six-pack.

She's from so far back in the holler, even their Presbyterians handle snakes.

She lives so far from the city she's got pet flies.

She's so country she uses cobwebs as party streamers.

He's so
country
he thinks
Deliverance
is a romantic
comedy.

Lord, what kind of hillbilly pill has she been chewing?

She's so country when she opens her mouth, sticks fall out.

That's more country than a chicken eatin' pork skins.

He lives so far out in the woods he has to head back to town to hunt.

They're so country if
they won the lottery they'd buy a
two-story double wide.

They live so far in the country
the sun sets between their
house and town.

They're so country they built a two-hole outhouse instead of a house.

They live so far in
the country they have to
pipe in sunshine.

He lives so far out I had to grease my engine twice 'fore I hit the main road.

It's over yonder!

They live out yonder in no man's land.

I live out yonder in podunk city.

Honey, he lives way out yonder in the boondocks.

I'm country as cornbread.

She's country as a tater salad sandwich.

He's country as goat nuts.

I'm country as a chicken coop.

I've got my truck jacked up higher than a camel's cootie.

The only thing that can heal my blues is some dirt road therapy.

Camouflage is my signature color.

Wanna go four wheeling?

Wanna go spotlighting?

Wanna go frog giggin'?

Wanna go fishin'?

Wanna go
to the lawn

mower

races?

Wanna hit the gun range
'fore church?

Do you love me as much as
you love hunting?

You don't need
six tree stands; you've only
got one ass!

Don't you dress
that deer in my garage!

Lord, we can't hang another deer in this den.

Reckon I can run my carburetor through my dishwasher?

Acknowledgments

First and foremost, I'd like to thank all y'all who supported my first book, *Talk Southern to Me*, and especially those who took the time to come meet me at book signing events throughout the South. I have boundless gratitude for fellow South Carolinian Queen Johnson, who generously helped organize so many of those book signings, and for all of the wonderful Southerners who hosted these events, fed me pimento cheese, and who continue to kindly sell my books in their stunning boutiques. I so appreciate all the love and support I've received from the folks in my hometown of Gaffney, South Carolina, and thanks to Will Armstrong, Bill Shepard, and their terrific team at Armstrong Public Relations for all their hard work and promotion.

Great bottomless thanks to the entire team at Gibbs Smith for the opportunity to write another book and to my brilliant editor, Katie Killebrew, for your guidance, support, and for having faith in my vision. To my literary agent, Berta Treitl, and her team at Renaissance Literary & Talent, I thank you for your contagious enthusiasm and for convincing me to write a book in the first place. And sincere appreciation must be given to the earliest believer in my writing, my long-time manager and friend Cindy Ambers and her spectacular team at Art/Work Entertainment. To the gifted screenwriter Caryn Lucas, I thank you for mentoring me and trusting my country-as-cornbread voice as a writer on your delightful Netflix comedy, *Country Comfort*.

I'm extremely grateful to the devoted fans of the Southern Women Channel who continue to motivate my creativity and propel my

Southern voice. Ginormous thanks must be paid to all those who have worked to help build my YouTube channel and to all the generous Southerners who have devoted their time and talent and appeared in my videos.

I am deeply and forever indebted to my Mama and Daddy who happen to be the finest and funniest Southerners I know. Thank you for raisin' me up right and for always encouraging me to follow my dreams and to embrace my Southern. You are my heart, my world, and my greatest inspiration. To the rest of my Fowler and Bonner family, please know I feel extraordinarily lucky to be blessed with your love and influenced by your Southern hilarity. Special thanks must be given to my Aunt Kathy Fowler for sharing her much-praised tater salad recipe; my cousin Angela Martin for sharing her medical expertise and countryfied remedies; and my cousin Dennis Fowler and his radio station, WZZQ (104.3 FM), for the boundless support and promotion.

Heartfelt thanks must be paid to my darlin' husband, Sam Sokolow, for smothering me with love, encouraging my artistry, and embracing all my Southern eccentricities. And to the rest of the Sokolow family, I thank you for your spectacular love and support and for politely tolerating my quirky Southern nature.

Finally, and most significantly, I'd like to thank my dearest Southern pals, Delaine Yates, Katherine Bailess, Sheila Hawkins, Alex Ellis, Logan Browning, Chasity Smith, Angie Schworer, Amy Timmons, Tim Smith, April Bender, Cindy Townsend, Leslie Fulmer, and Dana Pennington for your devoted friendship, love, and relentless humor. Y'all are funnier than a donkey on water skis and I love ya more than a skeeter loves blood.

South Carolina native *Julia Fowler,* is an actor, screenwriter, author, producer, and dancer who has worked in television, film, and on Broadway. She is the creator of YouTube's Southern Women Channel, home of the viral video series *Sh%t Southern Women Say*. She currently resides in Venice Beach, California, clear across the country from her beloved South . . . bless her heart. Visit her at www.southernwomenchannel.com.